PAY MATTERS

PAY
MATTERS

The Art
and Science *of*
Employee
Compensation

DAVID WEAVER

LIONCREST

PUBLISHING

PAY MATTERS

The Art and Science of Employee Compensation

ISBN 978-1-5445-1669-1 *Hardcover*

978-1-5445-1668-4 *Paperback*

978-1-5445-1667-7 *Ebook*

For my family who loves me,
my friends who support me,
my colleagues who sustain me,
and my students who reward me.

CONTENTS

INTRODUCTION

WHERE THERE'S SMOKE, THERE'S FIRE

"I can't live on what I'm making now," she said, holding back tears.

Her name was Sarah, and she was in her boss's office, giving him an ultimatum. She was in her early twenties at the time, and she'd been busting her butt for that company for over two years when she'd finally had enough.

She handed the CEO her personal budget, which included everything down to the penny...except for rent because she was living with her parents to make ends meet.

The CEO looked at her in surprise.

She said, "Do you think I'm doing good work for you?"

"Of course you are."

"Then why don't you pay me like it?"

Luckily, the CEO came to me to get help. I met with Sarah individually, and she showed me her budget the same way she did with the CEO. Now, I've been consulting people on compensation for decades, but Sarah was the first and only person I've ever worked with who was so desperate that she shared her personal budget with me.

Yeah, it was that bad.

Although she didn't have the experience to say it, what she was trying to communicate to her CEO and to me was, "I think I'm being paid below market, but I have no idea if that's right. All I know is that I can't live like this anymore."

With the CEO's help, I got my hands on her job description and did a market analysis. It turns out that her instinct was right: based on the market, she was underpaid by about $10,000 a year. She felt like she was underpaid, and she was. Where there's smoke, there's fire.

I took the results to the CEO.

"What do you think we should do?" he said.

"Pay her at market rate—give her the $10,000 increase."

"What if she leaves?"

"She's guaranteed to leave right now if you keep making her live like this. At least you'll have a chance if you give her the increase."

He gave Sarah the increase, and she was thrilled. Fast forward three years, and she was finally able to move out of her parents' house and buy a home of her own.

Sarah mustered a lot of guts to finally speak up about being underpaid. But what if she hadn't? And what about the months, or even years, that people in your organization are suffering in silence, all because they suspect they're underpaid, but don't speak up because they can't be sure?

You don't realize it until it's too late—when hardworking people like Sarah leave your organization, and you're left looking at the embers of their departure. You may never see the signals like smoke filling the office, alerting you to a fire you were never trained to see.

WHAT'S YOUR PHILOSOPHY?

More often than not, when people leave a company, it's because of compensation issues. Without a well-defined compensation program and a philosophy to drive it, you'll continue losing good people, and you'll continue to have no idea why.

But here's the kicker: even when people are paid well, if they don't know *why* they're paid well—because you don't have a definite compensation plan and haven't communicated it to them—they will still be dissatisfied.

Everyone assumes compensation expertise means you just run a bunch of numbers and do analysis. That's only partially true. It's as much art as it is science. There's a lot of judgment and independent decision-making involved, and yeah, it's a bit of analysis, but it's not what you think it is.

Don't let the math scare you. I'm going to demystify everything, including the numbers, to help you blend the science and art of compensation to become a compensation expert. I'm going to teach you how to analyze every job in your organization so you can find its equivalent in the external market, and how to use that information to incentivize your employees to get the happiest high-performers money can buy.

Are you ready to become a compensation expert?

CHAPTER 1

—— 8 ——

HOW IMPORTANT IS PAY?

HOW TO DEFINE YOUR COMPENSATION OBJECTIVES

"Pay isn't the most important thing in the world."

As an HR professional, you'd be shocked how often I hear that sentence. More often than not, that sentiment comes from people in leadership roles who don't have any immediate worries about their pay. But what's at the forefront of employees' minds when the unexpected happens?

What do people worry about when a natural disaster hits, like Hurricane Katrina? Or what about a global pandemic, or government employees in a shutdown, or a nationwide recession when people get laid off and go from steady paychecks to applying for unemployment?

They're not thinking about whether they like their manager or whether they have free massage days once a month at the office. They're thinking, *"When will I see another paycheck?"* (This may come immediately after their thoughts of health and their family's safety, but I'd argue that their next paycheck is directly tied to that as well.) When our livelihoods are threatened, we're faced with the stark reality that in all actuality, pay *is* the most important thing for employees. It's the tool that allows your employees to do everything else they need to do.

From a leadership perspective, pay is actually the most important thing in the world to your business. Why? Because compensation is the number one cost in your organization. When you think about it, nothing even comes close. Benefits might come second, and inventory might be a close third, but payroll is the horse to beat.

Inevitably, that puts you at odds with your employees; you want to control the cost of labor to make your company as profitable as possible, but your employees (understandably) want to make more money. It's a problem that every organization faces. But it's a necessary problem to solve. In this chapter, I'll give you an overview of the perfect compensation system. That way, you'll have a full understanding of the big picture before we get into the details. What are the details? How to solve the compensation problem so you can strike a payroll balance that works best for you *and* your employees.

THE PERFECT COMPENSATION SYSTEM

Throughout this book, I'll help you develop a perfect compensation system. Well, let me rephrase that—because compensation is as much art as it is science, I'll help you develop a *near*-perfect system. This system is based on four pillars of policy decisions. They are:

1. **Internal Consistency**—This involves collecting information about the nature of specific jobs in your organization and compiling documents that describe those jobs. It also requires you to compare jobs and order them from high to low based on the value they provide to your organization.

2. **External Competitiveness**—This is a process by which you do a market analysis to establish a pay policy. That process requires you to do salary surveys and compare your internal rates to external salaries in other organizations.

3. **Employee Contributions**—This part of the system requires you to review your employees' performance against well-defined performance standards, both in your industry and within your organization. Based on those standards, you will also create a process that rewards people based on merit, rather than seniority, gender, or other biased metrics.

4. **Administration**—Nailing the administration pillar allows you to plan for salary increases and more employees. It also includes a process to review your

payroll budget, evaluate your employees, and communicate the system clearly and effectively.

As we go through this book, I'll help you develop all four pillars of your compensation plan. By the end, you will have mastered all fourteen aspects of the four-pillar compensation model:

PILLAR 1: INTERNAL CONSISTENCY
Job Analysis
Collecting information about the nature of specific jobs through the use of questionnaires, checklists, observation, or interviews.

Job Descriptions
Documents that identify and describe jobs as they are currently performed.

Job Evaluation
A system used to compare jobs and establish pay differences among jobs in an organization.

Job Structure

An ordering of your organization's jobs from high to low based on their content or relative value to the organization.

Pay Philosophy

Establishment of a pay policy to lead, meet, or lag the external market relative to product, industry, or people competitors.

PILLAR 2: EXTERNAL COMPETITIVENESS

Salary Surveys

Participation in credible salary surveys to collect competitive market pay data.

Market Analysis

A comparison of internal rates of pay to external salaries to determine competitive position in the market and planned salary spending.

Salary Ranges

Internal pay guidelines with minimum, midpoint, and maximum pay rates that approximate the salaries paid in the external market.

PILLAR 3: EMPLOYEE CONTRIBUTIONS
Performance Evaluation

In a pay-for-performance system, a process to determine an employee's work results against performance standards and job expectations.

Increase Guidelines

A process to allocate salary increase dollars based on standards, such as merit or seniority, applied consistently across individuals within the same job and organization.

Incentive Programs

Variable compensation that rewards an employee for goal achievement. Forms include short-term, long-term, individual, team, and group incentive plans.

PILLAR 4: ADMINISTRATION
Salary Planning

Budgeting and forecasting compensation costs for the next plan year.

Pay Communication

Regular communication to managers and employees so

they understand the compensation system and how pay is determined.

Program Review

Assess the compensation program's effectiveness with managers and employees on a periodic basis.

THE COMPENSATION MODEL

I visualize this four-pillar list as a matrix that I call the compensation model.

Policy Decisions		Compensation Models		
Internal Consistency	Job Analysis	Job Descriptions	Job Evaluation	Job Structure
External Competitiveness	Market Definitions	Salary Surveys	Policy Lines	Pay Structures
Employee Contributions	Performance Based	Seniority Biased	Merit Guidelines	Incentive Programs
Administration	Planning	Budgeting	Communicating	Evaluating

You have to get each of those four policy decisions in place and ready before you can go to the next one. For example, we'll start the process by creating some internal consistency. That means you have to get your job analyses, job descriptions, job evaluations, and job structures in place before you can analyze external competitiveness.

Once you have your internal factors (such as job descriptions) consistent, you are in internal alignment. Only then can you look at the external market. Once you're internally aligned, you have to make sure you're externally competitive. Only then will you look at how competitively you pay your employees relative to the outside world.

You will then define your market based on multiple factors that we'll go into later, and then you will obtain salary survey data to do a comparison of your internal salaries and the market averages for each job. Based on your pay philosophy, you'll adjust your current salaries to match your market comparisons.

Then it will be time to build your base salary program, your incentive program, and your other rewards programs based on the employees' contributions to the company.

At this point, you'll have to decide if you'll be a performance-based or seniority-based compensation company. About 80 percent of organizations have performance-based pay systems, which I am in total agreement with. However, there are certain organizations that still rely on seniority-based compensation systems, such as government entities, unions, and universities.

SENIORITY-BASED PAY

There are a lot more negatives than positives for seniority-based compensation. Longer time in a job does not necessarily equate to higher performance. I've seen the side effects of a seniority-based pay program a lot working with high-level universities in the Boston area. Nowadays, these administrations want to move on from seniority-based pay to a performance-based system, because they realize that their higher-level employees are leaving. Why? Because high-performing new employees know they're performing at a high level, but their compensation isn't commensurate with their performance.

As more universities hire leaders from the private sector, we're seeing more colleges and universities demand this change, and it has some interesting results. For example, a businessman named Jim Luther was the co-founder of one of the largest biotechnology companies in the US. He eventually left the business and became president of an art school. In other words, he went from a performance-based industry to a seniority-based system, and he wanted to change it.

As his consultant, I helped him make that change, and there was so much resistance to it that it took three years to fully implement (that's the level of resistance you can face with compensation changes).

But after his school changed to performance-based compensation, they watched productivity take off—everything from developing curriculums to organizing events were being done more efficiently. Tasks that used to take years to accomplish were now getting done in a single semester, all with a lower budget and higher quality.

That's the power of moving from a seniority-based system to a performance-based system.

After you choose whether you will be seniority-based or

performance-based, it's time to evaluate every job in your organization. It's a tedious process, but think of it like building a home: you have to get the foundation of the structure in place before you can decorate the living room.

When I teach this stuff in my classes, the HR reps in attendance all groan when I tell them this, and for good reason. It's a lot of work to document and analyze every job—especially if you have dozens, hundreds, or even thousands of jobs in your organization. And maybe your organization is so large that you don't have any structure around compensation. I'm telling you, though, I've seen it time and time again: when you don't have any structure, you wind up discriminating against people. Inadvertently or not, you wind up paying people doing the same job differently, and if you have a man and woman doing the exact same job, and you haven't done your analysis, 96 percent of the time the person being paid less is the female employee.

This is important, and it's why more and more states have gender pay equity laws. If you don't do this analysis from the ground up, you will find yourself in legal trouble.

GENDER PAY EQUITY LAWS

As the laws change, so must your organization. For example, California passed a law that said if a job candidate asks to see your salary ranges, you have to reveal them. That means candidates across California are all asking to see those ranges, so if you haven't done the infrastructure work to figure that out, you're not going to be in compliance with the law.

This isn't just happening in California. As time goes on, more and more states are going to pass gender pay laws to help close that gap. And those gender pay issues start at the initial job offer. Here's what often happens:

Let's say a woman makes $10,000 a year less than her male counterpart in the same job. They both get "standard" 3.5 percent increases over the course of the next ten years. Does that do anything to close the gap? No. Let's say the female employee leaves that organization and tests out the open market. What's the first thing her potential employers ask her during interviews?

After they dance around the issue for a while, they'll ask her what her salary was at her old place of employment. She'll tell them the number that is below her market rate. But *because* she was undercompensated, her new employer will also undercompensate her, because she's been conditioned to think that's all she deserves. It's a damn shame, and for the moment, a lot of companies can get away with it. But as these new laws pop up, you won't be able to pay people less than they're worth and stay compliant.

SALARIES SHOULD BE AN OPEN BOOK

Here's how most companies go about salary negotiation: you ask what the candidate is making, what their expectations are, or what they want. Then they're in the uncomfortable position of trying to navigate answering that question.

What I'm advocating is that instead of putting the onus on the potential employee, I'll teach you how to create a proper salary range for every job in your organization, so you can say, "The salary range is between $80,000 and $100,000. We expect you to start out around $90,000. Does that work for you?" And even better, you should put the range directly on the job listing, so everyone is clear on what they're getting into without you, the employer, ever needing to know what your candidates are currently making.

But it's funny, you know? There are a lot of people who have a vested interest in keeping the salary negotiation one-sided. Recruiters are a great example. I get so many recruiters coming to me saying, "How can I negotiate the best situation for our employers if we don't know what people are making? I can't do my job!"

It's really simple. Just figure out what the value of the job is to you, the organization, and how much you're willing to pay for someone to do it, and don't worry about what candidates are making. If it's not enough money for them, they won't apply. It's simple and obvious, which means you'll look like a genius if you actually do it.

THE BEST PERSON AT THE LOWEST PRICE

I was presenting for twenty CEOs who wanted me to talk to them about the gender pay equity legislation. I went into detail about what's prohibited, including asking about people's pay history (because that tends to discriminate against women for the reasons we outlined above). I went into the recently passed pieces of legislation, which prohibited them asking people's salary histories in job interviews.

You know what they did? They groaned.

I groaned back at them. "What's the matter? This is good for you, your employees, and for candidates—everyone wins."

Their response was very interesting. "This is just more regulation," one of them said. "More compliance, more rules. We're sick of it."

I tried to explain again, but someone raised their hand and said, "I don't care if someone is male or female, I just want the best person at the lowest price."

Luckily, there were a few women in the room, one of whom pounded her hand on the table emphatically and said, "You guys don't get it. It's not about low-balling the best person. It's about paying the best person the market rate."

She certainly shut up the room. Most of those CEOs had

it wrong, and so do many other companies. This isn't just another compliance "issue" you have to deal with. This is about paying people the salaries they deserve.

And from your perspective, I get it: salary is the number one cost in your organization, so there's a constant compensation struggle between leadership and employees. But low-balling people and trying to get the best people for the lowest cost is not only hurting your employees. It's discrimination, which hurts everyone...including you.

A FEW COMPENSATION PLAN CONSIDERATIONS

Your compensation program should have a few elements in place before going into effect:

- It should reflect your organization's strategies.
- It should reinforce your business strategies.
- It should fit environmental and regulatory pressures.
- It should reflect your culture and values.
- It should consider your employees' needs.

What do I mean by all that? Let's say you have a so-called "hot job" you need to hire for, such as a security or data analyst, which is in high demand and, therefore, difficult to hire for. Your compensation system is a huge means by which you will attract people into that hard-to-recruit-for position. If you see that you're having trouble attracting talented people, you can use your compensation program to reel them in. A great compensation program is like putting better bait on your line to reel in the bigger fish.

> I've seen it time and time again; if an organization has a high turnover rate, the most likely explanation is that it's behind the market. You can fix the manager, and change other conditions, but nine times out of ten, if there's a high turnover rate, I can cut it at least in half by getting the compensation right.

HOW YOUR COMPENSATION PLAN REFLECTS YOUR CULTURE

It might sound harsh, but it's true: every organization thinks it's special and unique. Unfortunately, that's not true. If I had a dime for every time I heard that, I'd be a very rich man. "Oh, but we actually are different," you'll say next. Then I'll say, "Oh, really? Because I was just at another organization that does the same thing you do, and they said the same thing."

I hate to burst your bubble (Oh, who am I kidding? I love it.), but your organization is not unique. And even if you are, you are not so unique that you don't have to worry about being strategic about your compensation program. Nowhere in your culture does it explicitly say you should be haphazard with pay.

A software developer is a software developer, no matter

what your organization is. The job is not going to change drastically no matter where you are. Even if your mission is different than most companies, the work is roughly the same, so if you pay behind market, you'll experience turnover, no matter how unique you think you are.

HOW TO LOSE YOUR EMPLOYEES

> On average, replacing an employee costs two to three times the lost person's salary.

When I oversee exit interviews for roles, the top two reasons people leave are:

- Pay
- Opportunity (or lack thereof)

Why do they feel a lack of opportunity? Most top management teams want a flat organization, meaning they want to contain costs by not having multiple levels. From a strict dollars-and-cents perspective, that might *seem* to work, but from an employee's standpoint, they need to feel like they're advancing. And there's nothing that screams growth like a flat organization...right? Not so much. So those opposite needs—to contain costs from management and to advance in the role for employees—will always be at odds.

In most roles, I see organizations delineate three levels: entry, intermediate, and senior. In my experience, that's not enough opportunities for advancement to spark people's need for growth and development. I suggest four to six levels in each job. People want promotions, and they want more responsibility. So rather than looking at it as a larger cost for you, look at it as saving money by keeping them on board and teaching them to bring the organization more value, which leads to you paying them more.

> I've seen organizations with 70 percent turnover in a position cut it down to 30 percent with a 10 percent adjustment to compensation. That's an incredible return on investment.

LOOK THE PROBLEM IN THE FACE

When an organization experiences high turnover, everyone wants to look at everything but the pay. They say it's not a math issue; it's a human dynamics issue. Those employees weren't happy with the management. They weren't happy with the lack of parties. They wanted more office massage days. None of that is true. It *is* a math issue. People can feel when they're being underpaid.

So when you go through the steps in this book, and then go to them, look them in the face, and say, "We looked at the market, and we're making a 10 percent adjustment to your salary to meet the market rate," they'll not only appreciate that, but it will foster loyalty in them. You admit your mistake and you take steps to rectify it.

Having said that, there is an art to getting everything right. Throughout his book, I'll give you some formulas and math advice, but in the end, it'll be up to you to choose which strategies to employ, which ones to ignore, and which ones to make on your own.

You still have time to pay your people what they're worth. But as time goes on, you won't be able to make that choice anymore. As equal pay legislation gets passed, the choice will be made for you.

Let's talk about the legalities of compensation.

CHAPTER 2

8

YOU'RE NOT EXEMPT FROM RESPONSIBILITY

HOW TO HANDLE LEGAL ISSUES IN COMPENSATION

Paying people fairly isn't just the law—it's the right thing to do, and it's the best thing for your organization.

In this chapter, I'll go over some legal considerations for your compensation program, including recent (and not-so-recent) legislation that you should be familiar with. Let's start with the most impactful one: the Fair Labor Standards Act.

WHY YOU NEED TO KNOW ABOUT THE FAIR LABOR STANDARDS ACT (FLSA)

The FLSA was passed in 1938, and it hasn't changed much since then. It came about to ensure companies didn't abuse their employees, particularly their employees in low-level hourly positions. It limits the number of working hours, it establishes a minimum wage, it protects educational opportunities for youth (meaning it keeps young people from focusing on work instead of going to school), and it defines which employees are exempt from overtime pay and which employees are entitled to overtime pay. We'll get into more details on exemption and how it's determined in a few minutes but very briefly:

- Nonexempt Employees
  - In general, these are your hourly employees, and they are given protections such as minimum wage, overtime pay, and maximum hours worked.
- Exempt Employees
  - These are the employees on salary who are not entitled to overtime pay.

On the one hand, it's fortunate that the FLSA is still in place today because people need it. On the other hand, it's sad that it's still necessary and relevant, but, sadly, many businesses still try to circumvent labor laws. Don't be one of those businesses.

EXEMPTION CRITERIA

In order to be exempt from the FLSA (and not be eligible to earn overtime), an employee must satisfy three criteria:

- **Salary Level**—The employee must earn a minimum of $684 per week (or $35,568 per year).
- **Salary Basis**—The employee must be paid on salary, not hourly.
- **Job Duties**—The employee must perform certain executive, administrative, and professional job duties.

THE EXEMPTION TEST

The first two criteria are very objective, and therefore leave no room for interpretation. The third criteria is where people get mixed up. Here's how to test if your employee is exempt for administrative reasons:

- First of all, a job that is exempt from overtime will likely take place in an office, and will not consist of heavy manual labor. It will, instead, be directly related to managing or running business operations.

- It does not include working on a production line or selling a product in a retail or service establishment.
- The primary duty includes exercising discretion and independent judgment with significant business matters.

Here's a common job that trips people up when determining exemption status: administrative assistant. You could argue that it's an office job where you're assisting someone with running the business, so it should be exempt from overtime, right? But the difference is right there in the job title: they're *assisting* with the operation of the business, not doing it themselves. Moreover, they have to exercise discretion and independent judgment with matters of significance in order to be exempt. The administrative assistant doesn't fit that description, so they will *not* be exempt from overtime and would, therefore, be entitled to time-and-a-half overtime pay.

To ensure you're in compliance with the FLSA exemption laws, you should go to the Department of Labor website and run every job in your company through the exemption tests found here: dol.gov/agencies/whd/flsa.

Don't have time to run the exemption test for every job? The best alternative is to have an unbiased third party take a look to give you an outsider's perspective.

EXEMPTION IS NOT A STATUS SYMBOL

A lot of managers prefer their team to be exempt because they see it as a status symbol. It's proof that your team is not hourly, blue-collar workers. It's a very misguided notion. If your employees are getting exempt status and they shouldn't be, they are not only being robbed of their earned overtime pay, but you also put yourself in legal trouble.

It doesn't make sense when you think about it: it's not just the legal trouble that should worry you. It doesn't make financial sense either. If you get caught fraudulently paying non-exempt employees as exempt employees (meaning you're not giving them their earned overtime), the money you save from underpaying them will almost certainly come back to bite you in the form of lawsuits, fines, and back pay.

Here's a perfect example...

INSIDE SALES—EXEMPT OR NONEXEMPT?

Inside sales reps take inbound calls from customers and qualify those leads, putting them into their CRMs and sending those leads to the outside salespeople. Now, outside salespeople, as you know, are highly compensated with both salary and commissions. Unlike inside salespeople, who talk to customers over the phone, outside salespeople meet directly with customers face-to-face.

Now, the department of labor has made it very clear that outside salespeople are exempt from overtime pay. However, inside sales are usually nonexempt, which means they are eligible for overtime.

So from the manager's perspective, if you have a national company with thousands of salespeople across multiple time zones, you might be in trouble if you have offices full of inside salespeople taking inbound calls from customers, doing casual overtime beyond forty hours a week, and not getting compensated at time-and-a-half.

That's when I come in and have a hard conversation with them. After reviewing the sales jobs I tell them, "You need to reclassify these inside sales roles before one of them makes a complaint and the Department of Labor comes around. They won't just fine you. They'll force you to make back payments, too. Fix this, and give your inside salespeople their overtime pay."

Without fail, they'll say, "We don't have the budget for that!"

And every time I'll respond, "Do you have the budget to get fined six figures plus back pay?"

The answer is, of course, no. Then they'll take one final swing: "Our inside salespeople can't get all of their work done in less than forty hours a week."

"Then you either need to add more people, or you need to split people's shifts. Whatever it is, you have to fix it."

These fines are no joke. Take them seriously.

COMMON FLSA VIOLATIONS INCLUDE:

- Misclassifying employees.
- Overlooking off-the-clock work.
- Failing to pay unauthorized overtime.
- Not tracking breaks properly.
- Keeping inaccurate or incomplete records.
- Not compensating interns or volunteers.
- Failing to stay updated with regulations.

SOME EXPENSIVE FLSA LAWSUITS:

- FedEx paid $240 million in unpaid overtime.
- Walmart paid $62 million for forcing employees to work through breaks.
- MetLife paid $50 million for unpaid overtime.
- TGI Fridays paid $19 million for shortened wages.
- Victoria's Secret paid $12 million for unpaid call-in shifts.
- GNC paid $9 million because they didn't keep complete records of employee hours.

Ignorance of the law is no excuse, and it won't hold up in court. Make sure you look at your business practices and classify your employees properly.

Here are a few other pieces of legislation you should be familiar with as a compensation expert:

SHERMAN ANTITRUST ACT OF 1890

This law came about to fight monopolies and preserve a competitive business environment. Its impact on you is that in order to have a safe harbor, your salary survey sources must meet these criteria:

- The salary survey is managed by a third party.
- The information provided to survey participants is based on data more than three months old.
- There are at least five organizations reporting data, and no individual organization's data represents more than 25 percent of the sample.
- The salary data must be aggregated so you cannot identify the compensation paid by any particular organization.

EQUAL PAY ACT OF 1963

This act serves as an amendment to the FLSA and applies to everyone covered under its umbrella of protection. It's the first antidiscrimination law that directly relates to women and mandates equal pay for equal work. It says that you can only differentiate wages based on:

- A seniority system.
- A merit system.
- A system that measures earnings by quantity or quality.
- Any factor except biological sex.

CIVIL RIGHTS ACT OF 1964

Otherwise known as Title VII, this act expanded on the Equal Pay Act of the previous year. It expanded protections from discrimination to include discrimination based on:

- Race
- Color
- Religion
- Sex
- National origin

It also identified unlawful treatment in the form of disparate impact and disparate treatment, meaning as an employer, you are responsible for both the discriminatory treatment and the impact of that treatment on your employees.

COMPARABLE WORTH

Although there was no specific "comparable worth" legislation, this is a concept that came as a result of the antidiscrimination legislation of the sixties, and by the late seventies, we started recognizing the historical pay differences between men and women. Its premise is that men and women holding different jobs should be similarly compensated if the jobs require comparable skills, training, effort, and responsibility.

AMERICANS WITH DISABILITIES ACT OF 1990

This act prohibits discrimination against qualified individuals with disabilities, either physical or mental, in all aspects of employment, including:

- Hiring
- Firing
- Promotion
- Layoffs
- Recruiting

If a person is capable of performing essential job functions, the employer must provide reasonable accommodation, meaning they make adjustments to the work environment that permits a qualified employee with a disability to perform the essential functions of the job.

LILLY LEDBETTER FAIR PAY ACT OF 2009

This law reinstates prior equal pay laws and allows employees to make discrimination claims when:

- They receive a discriminatory paycheck (as in a paycheck that is less than what it should be due to their sex, race, national origin, age, disability, or religion).
- They receive a discriminatory pay decision (such as not getting an earned promotion).
- A discriminatory pay practice is adopted.

- A person is affected by the decision or practice of a pay program.

ONCE YOUR LAWYER'S HAPPY...

The stakes are high when it comes to legal considerations in compensation. Make sure you have these laws in mind as you move forward with this book. Before you can describe a job to a federal agent coming in to assess whether to fine you for noncompliance, you must first be able to describe the job to yourself and to your employees. If you're ready to proceed (legally, of course), it's time to analyze your jobs and write your job descriptions.

CHAPTER 3

8

CONSISTENCY IS KEY

HOW TO DO JOB ANALYSIS AND CREATE JOB DESCRIPTIONS

This chapter will be split into two parts: first, I'll teach you how to analyze all of the jobs in your organization, then I'll teach you how to use that data to create accurate job descriptions.

Let's start with the job analysis...

EIGHT STEPS FOR EFFECTIVE JOB ANALYSIS

1. Obtain management approval.
2. Inform employees.
3. Identify resources.
4. Decide your collection method and collect data.
5. Document the analysis.
6. Review for legal compliance.
7. Obtain approvals.
8. Outline procedures for staying up-to-date.

WHAT IS JOB ANALYSIS?

Simply put, job analysis is the set of steps you take to systematically obtain, categorize, and document any relevant information about a specific job. It sounds easy, right? But for those of you who have gone through this process, you know it's not nearly as simple as it sounds.

For one, employees don't like to be asked about their jobs. They are, of course, the best source of information for you when it comes to job analysis, but many managers hesitate to get them involved in the job analysis process.

Employees don't like being asked about their jobs because they're concerned that by digging into the specifics of their job, you're planning to lay them off, demote them, or reprimand them. There's a lot of fear there. That's what makes it so important to communicate this stuff. People need to know that you're not looking to fire them—if anything, you want to understand what they do in case you need to give them a raise.

> ### THE IMPORTANCE OF JOB ANALYSIS
>
> In short, job analyses can do the following for you:
>
> - Help you document work methods and processes for training purposes.
> - Provide a basis for performance evaluations.
> - Identify job families and career paths.
> - Identify job qualifications.
> - Determine if a job needs to be changed or updated.
> - Develop a job-worth hierarchy.
> - Assist with legal and regulatory compliance.

THE JOB ANALYSIS PROCESS

When most people get around to doing job analyses, they often don't have a process in place. A manager will stop an employee at the water cooler, and between casual conversations about Netflix and their weekend plans, the manager will say, "Hey, could you write up what you do for me? Nothing serious, just a sentence or two."

The problem is if you ask people to just write down what they do, their answers will be all over the place. You need to follow a strictly defined process that gets to the heart of the job. You need to discover the essential duties of the job, the minimum qualifications, necessary education, experience, skills, certifications, and if there are any physical, mental, or environmental factors that are necessary to perform the duties (to make sure it's in compliance with the Americans with Disabilities Act).

Having a consistent and defined process keeps you from getting a hodgepodge of answers and ensures that you're legally compliant. Keeping everything standardized also helps you match and compare your organization's jobs with those in other organizations.

But before you start asking people questions about their jobs, make sure you tell them exactly what's going on.

THE IMPORTANCE OF COMMUNICATION

I was teaching a fifteen-week course for people in human resources. One of my students was a human resources generalist named Sandra, who worked in an organization with about 300 people. The organization had never done any job analyses, so they had no job descriptions, no documentation, no process—nothing. Well, during one of our classes, I handed everyone a job analysis questionnaire that they could use as a template to do job analyses in their organizations.

Sandra got riled up as she held that template in her eager hands. She imagined going into her company, slapping this bad boy on everyone's desk, and earning the praise of senior management.

Unfortunately, it didn't happen like that. Quite the opposite.

The very next day, she went into work and sent that questionnaire to all 300 employees in the building. She didn't consult with the CEO, talk to her boss, or get any support from management whatsoever. She just sent that questionnaire out and hoped for the best.

Chaos ensued. The employees had no idea what this questionnaire was about—they didn't know if they were being fired or pranked—and because she hadn't communicated any of this with upper management, they didn't know what to make of the situation, either. It was a disaster.

Here's what really killed me in this whole thing: she was a student in my Tuesday/Thursday class. I gave out the template on a Tuesday. She sent the questionnaire that Wednesday, and she got in trouble Wednesday night. Then she came into class on Thursday and said, "Professor Weaver, you got me in trouble with that template."

"Already?" I said. "The ink on it is barely dry. What happened?"

"Well, I sent it to everyone in our company. Then my boss asked me what possessed me to send this questionnaire without telling anyone. I said, 'We don't have job descriptions for any of our 300 people, so I'm constantly being barraged by people asking questions that could be solved by doing this job analysis. My professor, David Weaver, said it was important, so I did it.'"

"Yes, but I didn't tell you to send it out *without management support*."

"I got that now, but I almost got fired."

Luckily, Sandra wasn't fired. She patched everything up with management and learned from her mistake. Now, fifteen years later, she's the VP of a giant food services organization, so she must have learned a lot.

But don't make the same mistake she did; don't do any of this job analysis work without first getting support from management and communicating the purpose of it to your organization's employees. It's such a sensitive topic, and people may feel that their livelihoods are threatened. Do everyone a favor and make sure your company leaders are on board.

REMEMBER THE LEGAL CONSIDERATIONS

Yes, I'm harping on this again. There are many legal considerations to take into account when doing job analyses, but the most common and prominent ones are:

- Equal pay.
- Equal employment opportunity (EEO).
- Affirmative action.
- Americans with Disabilities Act (ADA).
- Fair Labor Standards Act of 1938 (FLSA).

The best way to stay in accordance with these laws is by ensuring that you get detailed information in the job analysis process. That way, when you move on to doing job descriptions, you are describing the most essential duties. If you overinflate the qualifications required to perform a job, you inadvertently screen out people who might be qualified. If you discriminate (no matter how inadvertently) against certain people due to overinflating the job requirements, you leave yourself open to more legal troubles.

So it's important to get high-quality data. The data you collect will relate to what is commonly referred to as compensable factors—these are the four things your organization pays people for:

- Their level of skill.
- Their level of mental and physical effort.
- Their level of responsibility and accountability.
- Their working conditions.

HAZARD PAY

If someone has adverse working conditions—such as working in the sun all day or working in a walk-in refrigerator—they are entitled to higher compensation. Most organizations don't take adverse working conditions into account, but if you want to be a compensation expert, you have to. That's why you have to have good data on working conditions—if you don't get that information now, then you may not compensate people appropriately for their conditions, and you could be liable for legal action.

> ### NEW HAZARDS
>
> When a public health crisis sprang up, we saw grocery store cashiers and other essential workers get hazard pay. They were being forced into working conditions that were more dangerous than what they'd originally agreed to, so they were given more compensation as a result, recognizing that their working conditions had become more hazardous.

Getting good data on job information starts by deciding what source you'll get it from.

YOUR POSSIBLE SOURCES FOR JOB INFORMATION

In a highly-efficient organization, ideally, you'd be able to get all of this accurate and up-to-date data by simply walking into HR and asking for it. Unfortunately, if you work in HR, you know that's rarely the case. You have to collect that data yourself, through any combination of these three methods:

1. DIRECT OBSERVATION

This entails watching an employee do their job and looking for patterns in what they do over time. Now, this only works for nonexempt, production-related jobs, such as assembly-line employees, so it's a very limited data collection method.

If you want to use this method, the procedure looks like this:

- You meet with the manager to identify the best employees to observe.
- You explain to the employee what you're doing before you start observing (otherwise they feel like they're being watched like a zoo animal and won't know why).
- Review the existing job description (if any) before observing.
- Conduct a follow-up meeting to review your job documentation with the employee.
- Verify the job duties with the supervisor or manager.

Advantages	Disadvantages
Opportunity to gain firsthand knowledge of job opportunities	Can be costly in terms of time and resources
Omissions or exaggerations are less likely to occur	"Big Brother" syndrome
Ability to personally see and experience working conditions/envirnonment	Can disrupt the employee
Opportunity to ask questions/ clarify responses	Can be misleading

The main advantage of using direct observation is that it gives you the opportunity to gain firsthand knowledge of the job responsibilities. That means omissions or exaggerations are less likely to occur (nobody can say they manage the whole production floor if you watch them work as an individual contributor on the assembly line). It also gives you the chance to ask questions in the moment while the work is being done.

On the other hand, it can be costly and gives people the sense that Big Brother is watching, which can disrupt the employee and make them think they're on the chopping block.

2. QUESTIONNAIRES

I strongly advise that you use employee questionnaires to do your job analyses. They can be very efficient and can produce great results, but they do take a lot of time to prepare.

And if you rely on open-ended questions, you may need some to be translated, and poor writing skills can affect the results.

Pro tip: let your employees fill out questionnaires without you being in the room with them, breathing down their necks.

Advantages	Disadvantages
Very efficient	Can be very time consuming to prepare
Flexible	Poor writing skills can affect results
Can produce more successful results	May have to be translated

No matter what form your questionnaires take, you'll notice that people will tell you about special projects they've been asked to do that aren't part of their normal job duties. They'll tell you about it because they're not being rewarded for it. They know that taking on more duties helps them get more exposure, helps them learn more, and improves their chance of developing, but they should be paid for that, and it's an organizational mistake not to (we'll get into this more in chapter 10 when I teach you about variable pay).

The point is, when you hand out questionnaires, be prepared for people to focus on special projects outside of their job scope. Just know that they want to be recognized and rewarded for them—and who could blame them?

3. INTERVIEWS

This method works really well, as long as you use a consistent format. My suggestion is that you do interviews in tandem with questionnaires.

There are three types of interviews:

Incumbent Interviews

These are great for all job types, and usually work like this:

- You explain the purpose of the meeting to the employee.
- You create a relaxing atmosphere.
- Start by asking broad, open-ended questions.
- Listen well and take notes.
- Maintain an objective viewpoint.
- Summarize the observations with the employee at the end of the meeting.
- Explain the next steps.
- Summarize the notes immediately after the interview.
- Verify the job duties with the incumbent's manager/supervisor.

Advantages	Disadvantages
Allows the incumbent to describe tasks and duties that are not observable	Incumbant may omit or exaggerate job duties
Flexible	Interviewee may focus on one area and neglect others
Allows job analysts to probe into the specific aspects of the job	Job interviewer may misinterpret work
Incumbent may be more comfortable	Requires more prep work than direct observation

These interviews are great because they allow the incumbent employee to describe the tasks and duties that are not observable and allow you to probe into specific aspects of their job. It's a very flexible format, too, which can make you and the employee much more comfortable.

On the other hand, because you're not directly observing what the employee does, they may omit or exaggerate their job duties, and they may focus on one area of their job and neglect others. It also leaves a lot more up to your interpretation, and it can require more prep work than direct observation.

Group Interviews

These interviews allow you to review job content with a group of employees. They're great for situations when individual interviews are impossible or impractical, such as when you don't have time to meet with each person. You'll go through the same guidelines as the individual interviews, but you'll also request that they fill out a job questionnaire first, which you'll review before the meeting to establish interview questions.

Advantages	Disadvantages
Same as individual interviews	Can become complaining session
May result in more comprehensive overview of job	Often dominated by one or more participants; some participants may be left out
More feedback is provided	Harder to pull together

The key here is to maintain control of the meeting—you may feel outnumbered. Using these group interviews may give you a more comprehensive overview of the job because you'll simply get more data points, but they can turn into complaining sessions that are dominated by one or more participants. These should only be used in the rarest of situations, such as when you don't have the capacity to do individual interviews.

Supervisor Interviews

Similar to the individual interviews, with supervisor interviews, you talk to the employee's supervisor, which can give you a more objective overview of the job. However, beware that it may lead to biased and inaccurate responses.

Advantages	Disadvantages
Same as individual interviews	Can be inaccurate
May result in more objective overview of job	Perspective can be biased

THE SCARY PART OF INTERVIEWS

Here's what often happens with interviews: I'll talk to the employee, I'll get data on everything they do, then I'll summarize that data and give it to the manager. You know what happens, time and time again? The manager is surprised. They'll say, "Oh, wow, I didn't know they were doing all that."

That's scary to me. Because when a director, supervisor, or manager doesn't know what their employee is doing, it means they aren't conscious of what duties and responsibilities they're obligated to. That means you're not compensating people for what they're doing *because you don't know what they're doing*. Once again, that can leave you open to legal trouble. It can also lead to duplication of efforts.

If somebody consistently completes one task that another person is supposed to be doing, they might both be doing the same thing unnecessarily (which happens more often than you'd ever care to think).

For example, in a lot of organizations, I'll meet someone who says they're in charge of training their coworkers and new hires. Then I'll bring that information to the top management team. I'll say, "In ten out of your twelve departments, you have someone who says they're responsible for training. But here's the thing: you already have a centralized training system that's supposed to take care of all of it."

How much money gets wasted in those duplicated efforts? Millions?

Other areas that are rife with people putting in duplicate efforts are:

- IT (non-IT people will go around fixing technology like you wouldn't believe).
- Finance and budgeting.

Getting this data does offer you a chance to reset expectations for what your employees should be doing, which is the whole idea behind performance appraisal. Otherwise, you'd be losing productivity on people doing what they were never hired to do.

In my experience, the incumbent interview method is best. You get to sit down with the employee and hear about their job straight from the horse's mouth. Group interviews are much less effective because you get so many varied opinions in one place.

The next best thing is supervisor interviews, but even those can be biased, particularly because many managers have never done the job they're supervising.

COST AND PRODUCTIVITY

You may be hesitant to put in the time and resources to do individual employee interviews with each and every person. It *is* expensive, but it's not nearly as expensive as never collecting the data in the first place. What you learn will more than pay for itself in gained productivity and avoided lawsuits.

And if you really need to cut costs, you can do the questionnaire only, which is the next best thing.

EXAMPLES OF QUESTIONNAIRES

There are two types of questionnaires: open-ended and highly structured.

There are advantages and disadvantages to both types. For the open-ended questionnaire, which asks people to answer in the form of a narrative, people may provide information that isn't useful. As such, your data won't be consistent. However, you may learn something you didn't know before and would have never asked in a highly structured questionnaire.

On the other hand, the highly structured questionnaire gives you a consistent data set because everyone is reading and responding to the same questions as the other respondents.

In both cases, what you're really asking people is, "Tell me why your job exists?" You do that by getting them to tell you what percentage of time each week they dedicate to major job duties and what qualifications are required to perform those functions.

Open-Ended	Highly-Structured
Please summarize the primary purpose of your job in four to seven sentences.	Job-related experience for competent performance of this job (check one). ☐ No experience required ☐ Up to one month ☐ Over 1 month, up to 12 months ☐ Over 1 year, up to 3 years ☐ Over 3 years, up to 5 years ☐ More than 5 years

HOW TO CREATE JOB DESCRIPTIONS

Now that you've collected the data and completed your job analyses, it's time to organize that data in the form of job descriptions.

A job description typically includes:

- The essential job functions.
- Qualifications, including necessary:
    - Education
    - Knowledge
    - Skills
    - Abilities
- Physical and other demands.
- Job duties.
- Reporting structure.
- Job family.
- Pay grade.

Although a good job description will include all of those elements, there is no universal format for a job description, primarily because it's not required by law. However, I highly recommend you have them (in fact, if you don't want to create job descriptions, you might as well put down the book now).

A job description should not overstate or understate the minimum requirements of the job.

One mistake I see in job descriptions is that HR reps and managers tend to describe the incumbent or the person doing the job rather than the job itself. I always tell people, 'The person's resume tells you about the person, and we don't really care about that for a job description." Some organizations try to get out of this by falling back on everyone's resumes. I say that's not helpful. You want the job to stand on its own without depending on the individuals to describe it for you.

WHY DO YOU NEED A JOB DESCRIPTION?

Job descriptions help you identify and attract qualified applicants. It also helps you ensure that you're in compliance with the Americans with Disabilities Act (ADA), and it helps you determine your FLSA classification with each job (as in whether it's exempt from overtime or not).

Job descriptions are essential tools for conducting job interviews, performance reviews, coaching and employee development, disciplinary procedures, and terminations. It is, quite literally, the basis for everything we do as compensation professionals. For example, if you have job descriptions laid out for every position in your organization, you can use them as a tool for development. You can show everyone in your organization what the next level up looks like for them, and what exactly they need to learn or do to get there.

It makes me scratch my head that more organizations don't do this. If you have explicit job descriptions for every role, it does wonders to create growth and motivation throughout your company.

Why would you let people walk out of your company to grow elsewhere? Let them grow with you. You've already put the time and resources into training them—it's far more expensive to hire someone new than it is to help someone you already have. People want a sense of growth and progression, and you can't present people with that map of progress without job descriptions.

> When people leave an organization, it's for two reasons: they want more money, or they want more growth opportunities.

A GOOD JOB DESCRIPTION

Here's an example of a high-quality, one-page job description for a common job: accountant.

Job Title: Accountant	Prepared By: Greg Larson
Department: Finance	Prepared Date: 6/2/20XX
Reports To: Manager of Accounting	Approved By: Erin Murphy
FLSA Status: Exempt	Approved Date: 6/13/20XX

JOB SUMMARY

Applies principles of accounting to analyze financial information and prepares income and balance sheet statements and reports. Maintains a computerized financial reporting system and audits the information for accuracy. May assign work to employees engaged in general accounting activities.

ESSENTIAL FUNCTIONS

- Compiles and analyzes financial information to prepare entries to accounts, such as general ledger accounts, and documents business transactions.
- Analyzes financial information detailing assets, liabilities, and capital, and prepares balance sheet, profit and loss statement, and other reports to summarize and interpret current and projected company financial position for managers.
- Audits contracts, orders, and vouchers, and prepares reports to substantiate individual transactions prior to settlement.
- Installs, modifies, documents, and coordinates implementation of accounting systems and accounting control procedures.
- Devises and implements systems for general accounting.
- Makes recommendations regarding the accounting of reserves, assets, and expenditures.
- Conducts studies and submits recommendations for improving the organization's accounting operation.

- Collects appropriate data and prepares federal, state, and local reports and tax returns.
- Performs other duties as assigned.

EDUCATION AND EXPERIENCE

Bachelor's degree in accounting or equivalent, and two to four years of related accounting experience required.

PHYSICAL, MENTAL, AND ENVIRONMENTAL REQUIREMENTS

Required to regularly sit. Occasionally required to stand or walk. Occasionally required to lift and/or move up to 25 pounds. Must be able to concentrate for extended periods of time, paying close attention to detail. Works in a normal office environment.

ARE YOUR QUALIFICATIONS JUSTIFIED?

When it comes to job qualifications, employers typically require certain knowledge, skills, aptitude, training, and previous experience. But companies tend to exaggerate what qualifications are actually needed, which deters potentially qualified individuals. To avoid this, make sure the qualifications stated in the job description have a direct relationship to the job functions. So, for example, a forklift driver won't need a college education or the ability to write clearly and effectively in English, so don't put that in the job description.

Let's go over some common job qualifications that are inadvertently discriminatory.

> All qualifications, including educational requirements, must be justified.

"MASTER'S DEGREE REQUIRED"

Not all jobs require a degree. You'll know if a qualification is justified if it's necessary for the job. That's it. A lot of companies put qualifications that aren't necessary for a job, such as educational requirements.

Here's a simple guideline

If you're asking for a certain level of education and experience, look at the people already performing the job. If you're asking for more education and experience than the people already doing it, then you're discriminating.

"DRIVER'S LICENSE REQUIRED"

A lot of employers ask employees to have a driver's license. Unless driving is required for the job—such as trucking—

that's discrimination. You're inadvertently screening out people who take public transportation.

Unnecessary (and Potentially Illegal) Phrasing

- "Great for a recent college grad"—That's a covert way of screening out older people.
- "Great opportunity for moms"—That's another way of discriminating without telling people it's part-time work during the day.

If you look through most job postings, you'll see these covert ways to discriminate against people based on age, race, and gender. Don't be one of those companies. Stick to what's necessary for the job, and you'll be fine.

JOB DESCRIPTION CONSISTENCY

Your job description will likely have a bit of marketing about the company up front (which is fine), but beyond that, every job description—both internally and externally—should be in a consistent format that sticks to the necessities of the job. That way, your candidates know exactly what they're interviewing for, rather than someone hopping on the phone and wasting your time applying for a job that they don't actually want, just because the description wasn't accurate.

"MAY PERFORM OTHER DUTIES"

My classes always get a kick out of this one: you want to include a bullet under the essential functions that says, "May perform other duties as assigned." Now why would you put that in a job description?

In short, it's a CYA move (i.e., a Cover Your Ass move). When you ask people to do special projects, you don't want them to come back and say it's above and beyond their job description. You can politely remind them to refer to their job description, where it says they may perform other duties as assigned.

Keep in mind: this isn't about taking advantage of your employees. Not at all. It's about making sure you're equipped with the knowledge to create a legal and comprehensive job description.

Now, having said that, this is not an excuse to abuse someone and pile on beyond their capabilities. Employees are often unsure about bringing this stuff up because they don't want to look like they're trying to squeeze the company for all it's worth. However, don't think that means you can squeeze your employees for beyond what you're compensating them for. Just cover your bases without exploiting your employees.

TITLE INFLATION

As far as job titles go, just be descriptive. Don't make a job sound like more than it is. Obviously, be politically correct and nondiscriminating, but avoid title inflation. Don't call someone the president of finance when they're the accounting supervisor. That doesn't help anybody.

A lot of CEOs and other business leaders refute that by saying, "Job titles are free, so why not embellish them to make people feel good?"

On the surface, it makes sense. But I see it bite people in the backside all the time. When you artificially inflate job titles, people think they deserve more compensation, even though their title has nothing to do with their pay. Job title inflation leads to ego inflation. And ego inflation leads to a desire to get paid beyond market rate. Squash that conversation before it ever starts by giving each job description an accurate title.

You're not hiring a beverage dissemination officer—you're hiring a bartender.

You're not hiring for an environmental improvement technician—you're hiring a custodian.

You're not hiring a director of first impressions—you're hiring an administrative assistant.

Those title inflations may make people feel good, but they set the wrong expectations for you, your employees, and your customers.

WHAT MAKES A BAD JOB DESCRIPTION?

A bad job description would be anything that's too long. I cringe when I do a market analysis for a company, and they give me a job description that's eight pages long. It's always full of fluff. One page is perfect, two is the max.

ONE LAST THING: THE APPROVAL DATE

I ask that you include the approval date because I recommend you don't use a job description that's more than three years old. That may seem like another unnecessary pain in the butt, but you can make the updating process relatively easy: update and reapprove each job description either when someone new fills the job, or when someone already in the job is up for review. That's a great way to recapture that data.

Or you can just update a third of your job descriptions every year, so they're all updated every three years.

No matter which approval and updating method you choose, all job descriptions should be filed in a centralized electronic database, rather than kept haphazardly in some folder collecting dust in the office.

WHAT'S NEXT?

We've collected the job analysis data, and we've created the job descriptions; now, we'll create an internal job hierarchy.

CHAPTER 4

RANK AND FILE

HOW TO EVALUATE AND ORGANIZE JOBS

Once you have your job analysis down and your job documentation figured out, now you can do your job evaluation. This is where you figure out the value of each job within your organization. We call this internal equity, and teaching you how to do that will comprise the first part of this chapter.

After you determine each job's internal equity, you'll determine where it corresponds to the job market. We call this external equity, and teaching you how to determine this will comprise the second part of this chapter.

Let's dig in.

INTERNAL EQUITY
YOUR BIGGEST COMPENSATION CHALLENGE

The biggest challenge with compensation is rewarding people appropriately for the services they're asked to provide, while at the same time containing labor costs (your biggest expense). It's a constant balancing act. Employees constantly solicit senior leaders for more money, and senior leaders always complain about greedy employees. You have to strike a balance.

Here's a secret: even if you do strike a balance, that tension never leaves. However, if that tension goes too far, that's when you see things like unions pop up so people can get paid competitively, get benefits, and have better working conditions.

You don't want to deal with a unionized workforce, do you? The answer is no. Your employees don't want to feel the need to unionize, either. So keep them satisfied, keep the senior leaders satisfied, and you'll all be happy.

THE ROI OF PAYROLL

Your goal here is to place a concrete value on every job in your organization and rank them in a hierarchy. This helps you optimize your return on investment for payroll because if you know exactly what people are doing, you can manage their tasks and duties and figure out how to pay them competitively.

HOW TO DETERMINE A JOB'S INTERNAL VALUE

- You can look at the content of the job and place a value on that relative to its importance in your organization.
- You can look at the individual in the job and place value on them.
- Or you can use some combination of the two.

Even if you have a lot of turnover, the value of any given job should be consistent. Of course you can (and should) pay individuals different amounts within a single job, based on their experience, education, and skills, but from my standpoint, it's best to focus on the value the job brings to the organization and compensate based on that. That should define the base salary, which you can supplement based on the individual's qualifications and performance.

Once you figure out what that value is, you can build a job structure that determines your internal hierarchy. Based on that internal hierarchy, you can start to compare your people to the external market.

THE TOOLS OF THE TRADE

You'll need some tools to determine your jobs' internal equity based on the four compensable factors: skill, effort, responsibility, and working conditions. Those tools are split into two categories: quantitative measurements and non-quantitative measurements.

Quantitative Measurements
Point Factor System

This system allows you to identify each job's compensable factors and assign them point values. The job value, therefore, is equal to the sum of the point values. This system is easy to use and allows you to consider and compare many subtle aspects of dissimilar jobs. However, it is unbelievably time-consuming and expensive to develop and maintain. And it is very difficult to reach a consensus on anything with this system (which we'll discuss more in a minute).

Nonquantitative Measurements
Job Ranking

Job ranking is simple: you look at every job in your organization and rank them from highest to lowest. This is a quick process and requires little training or investment to maintain. However, despite how easy it is to rank the top and bottom of your job hierarchy, ranking the middle proves to be a consistent challenge.

Advantages	Disadvantages
Quick and simple	Different perspectives lead to different results
Little training required	Can become an evaluation of the individual rather than the job
Inexpensive to implant and maintain	Has no documentation

For most companies, the CEO or president will be at the top. That's easy. Then you have a position like general manager. But once you move down from there, everything gets muddled. If you do choose this measurement method, I recommend using an alternating strategy to determine the middle of the hierarchy. Once you have the top and bottom established, choose the next highest job, then the next lowest job, and so on until you have as much of the middle placed as possible.

Note that this only works with a small organization with less than fifty jobs, and even then, it's very challenging.

Job Classification

This measurement asks you to slot your jobs based on pre-defined benchmark descriptors and match them as closely as possible.

Advantages	Disadvantages
Good when there are many jobs	Imprecise
New jobs can be evaluated easily	No job measurement
Easy for employees to understand	Force-fits jobs into existing categories

This method is good when you have a large number of jobs to measure. That's why government organizations love this tool. However, this method is imprecise and can force you to erroneously force-fit jobs into existing categories.

That's what happened with the TSA.

THE TSA'S CLASSIFICATION PROBLEM

My experience consulting the TSA is a perfect illustration of the imprecise nature of job classification measurements. It was just after 9/11, and the Transportation Security Administration was off to a rough start. As they attempted to roll out their entirely new agency, they struggled to hire and keep enough agents to stay afloat. To make matters worse, the security agents they did hire often left without explanation.

That's when—in one of the most surreal moments of my professional life—the TSA called me looking for help.

"We don't understand what's happening," an agency leader said on the phone. "We can't keep anyone. Can you take a look at our job descriptions and tell us if we're compensating these people correctly?"

I said, "I'll help you, but I'm not looking at your generic job descriptions."

He was a little surprised. Federal agencies don't look at market data to calculate their compensation. They have so many different jobs that they simply don't have the capacity to do that. Agencies like the TSA just look at the federal pay schedule descriptions and slot each job where it seems to fit best. It's a very imperfect art (at best).

Despite that standard practice, we'd have to change course if we wanted to help them retain more agents. I went to work researching other security jobs in the private market, figuring out what those employers paid their security agents, and told the TSA, based on my market research, where to slot their salaries.

I quickly discovered that other security positions with similar tasks and duties in private companies paid significantly more than the TSA was offering agents. No wonder they were leaving in droves.

Then, when I compared the market data with the federal pay schedule, I discovered the root problem: in the federal compensation slotting, the TSA was compensating its agents two slots below where they should have. That was a major difference.

Once we got those roles slotted at the appropriate compensation levels, the TSA was able to hire and keep far more employees than they did through their traditional federal categorization methods.

Government agencies don't have the capacity to look at market data, because they just have too many jobs and too many descriptions to categorize. I would guess there are a lot of government employees who are underpaid simply because of that.

The job classification method isn't the only measurement system with problems.

THE FLAWS WITH POINT FACTOR ANALYSIS

I've been doing point factor analysis for years, and I have to tell you: nobody ever reaches a consensus in a job evaluation committee. Ever. Some people are stingy with points, and other people are very generous. Either way, it's not as scientific as people think. People's biases come out and it's exacerbated further by their stubbornness.

Having said that, here's a sample point factor breakdown, including the weighting for every factor and job level:

Factor	1st Degree	2nd Degree	3rd Degree	4th Degree	5th Degree
SKILL					
1. Knowledge	14	28	42	56	70
2. Experience	22	44	66	88	110
3. Initiative & Ingenuity	**14**	**28**	**42**	**56**	**70**
EFFORT					
4. Physical Demand	10	20	30	40	50
5. Mental or Visual Demand	5	10	15	20	25
RESPONSIBILITY					
6. Equipment or Process	5	10	15	25	25
7. Material or Product	5	10	15	25	25
8. Safety of Others	5	10	15	25	25
9. Work of Others	5	10	15	25	25
JOB CONDITIONS					
10. Working Conditions	10	20	30	40	50
11. Hazards	5	10	15	20	25

Here's a sample description of the Initiative and Ingenuity factor, broken down by every degree:

INITIATIVE AND INGENUITY

This factor measures the independent action, use of judgment, making of decisions, and the amount of resourcefulness and planning required as determined by the complexity of the duties performed.

First Degree

Use of little judgment to follow instructions; use of simple equipment in performing duties with little or no choice as to the procedures used in achieving results.

Second Degree

Use of some judgment to comply with instructions or prescribed routines, methods, or practices involving the making of minor decisions.

Third Degree

Use of judgment to plan, perform, and make decisions related to the sequence of set-ups, operations, and processes within the limitations of recognized or standard methods and procedures.

Fourth Degree

Use of considerable judgment to plan and perform unusual and difficult work where only general methods are available, and the making of broad decisions involving considerable initiative and ingenuity.

Fifth Degree

Use of broad conceptual judgment, initiative, and ingenuity to work independently toward ultimate objectives on very involved and complex projects, and to devise methods and procedures to meet unusual conditions and to make original contributions to solve complex problems.

Advantages	Disadvantages
Easy to use	Time consuming and expensive to develop and maintain
Permits close shading of job values	Does not always link well to the market
Permits comparison of dissimilar jobs	How to weigh factors?
Considers many aspects of a job	Consensus

Now, obviously your organization can weight these factors differently based on which are most important for your company, but this is a good template if you choose to use it.

Point Inflation

In the old days, managers would notice an employee taking on extra responsibilities and appeal to a job evaluation committee. The manager asked if the added responsibility required a higher point value for the employee and subsequent pay increase. It seemed like an honest enough process.

But managers started embellishing the job descriptions for their employees so they could reach a higher pay grade. Because no organization would let an employee get paid more than their supervisor, the employee's pay increase would guarantee a pay increase for the manager, too (all fraudulently, by the way).

In short, the point factor system is a very involved, time-consuming, and expensive practice, and I don't recommend it. It used to be the go-to evaluation system, but over time we've transitioned away from it.

Instead, I recommend you determine your jobs' value based on market pricing.

EXTERNAL EQUITY
MARKET PRICING

This is the process of matching your jobs to the market and valuing them based on market pay practices. In other words, the market dictates your pay relative to the internal worth of your jobs.

Advantages	Disadvantages
Competitive pay practice	Difficult to directly compare many jobs
Simpler, may be less costly approach	Pay data may not be available

This is the method we used with the TSA. I would say this is the superior option to the other internal-based methods, but you can't use this method alone. Quite frankly, market pricing will work for about 60 percent of your organization's jobs, because you'll only be able to get data on benchmark (common) jobs.

Then there is about 40 percent of your jobs that will require you to use the other methods I mentioned in the first part of the chapter.

JOBS YOU CAN'T CATEGORIZE

Because you'll only be able to classify about 60 percent of the jobs, you'll have to approximate the rest, but it's not that tough. Here's how you do it: let's say you have a director of finance position that you found salary data for, you have a director of sales that you also have data for, but you have a director of sustainability position that you don't have market data for. The data for those positions are:

- Director of finance: $90,000.
- Director of sales: $92,000.

Because they're all from the same job category (director), you can use those two jobs as reference points to find the price for your director of sustainability position.

Just look at where that position fits in the hierarchy relative to those other two director roles. For example, if your director of sustainability sits in between those other two roles, you can reasonably infer that the position should be paid about $91,000. Easy, right?

PROPER MARKET PRICING

In order to do a proper market pricing analysis, you have to do two things:

Identify Your Marketplace

Consider the geographic area where you recruit candidates. How do you determine how wide your geographic marketplace is? It's interesting because as you go up the hierarchy of jobs, your marketplace distance grows. For example, an entry-level position would likely have something like a thirty-mile geographic market. Why? Because nobody will move across the state (or even across the city) to work an entry-level position.

However, a management position might be spread out to a more commutable distance, such as sixty miles. Once you get up to the executive level, the entire country might be part of your geographic marketplace, because a CEO would be willing to move across the city, state, region, or even country for a new position.

Identify Your Competitors

Make sure you know who your peer organizations are, including product, service, and people competitors.

Determine Your Data Sources

You want to make sure you're using data from reputable published surveys, such as trade or association surveys (we'll discuss this more in the next chapter). Tip: don't focus on surveys that use phone or email survey data.

WHY MARKETING IS UNDERVALUED IN THE MARKET

Internally, a head of marketing position will have a lot of relative value in a company, so the company will place that role high in the hierarchy. But externally, that role doesn't have as much external value. In fact, almost every time an organization I work with looks at the hierarchy we've created, they move the head of marketing (or similar role) higher in the organization.

It seems like a contradiction: if so many companies value this role internally, why doesn't the external market compensate to value it higher as well?

The answer is simple: it takes the market some time to catch up.

The same thing happened/is happening for data analysts and cybersecurity specialists. A few years ago, these jobs were undervalued or didn't exist in most companies. Now all large organizations have these roles and are catching up to compensate them accordingly.

It generally takes three years for the market (i.e., job survey results) to catch up to what most companies internally value each position.

MY RECOMMENDATION: USE MARKET PRICING

About 70 percent of organizations now use market pricing to analyze job data. And the only reason I even go through point factor, ranking, and classification is because I want you to know what's available, and the benefits and downfalls of each method of job evaluation. Moreover, you may need to create some combination of every method to do a complete job analysis of every role in your company.

If your company is hanging on to an old tool (most likely point factor analysis) and is unwilling to let it go, just know that there are better tools out there. You may need an outside consultant to set the system up and help you learn how to do it on your own, but once you have it, the time and money savings are incredible.

However, this is not a "set it and forget it" model. The same way you need to update your job descriptions every three years, you also need to keep up with the market trends and update your salaries consistently (at least annually), because once your system lags behind the market, you'll suddenly start losing employees and have no idea why, just like the TSA.

WHY ARE YOU HANGING ON?

Some people want to hang on to the old methods of analysis because they feel their jobs depend on it. I knew one client who insisted on evaluating every single job on the basis of experience. I had to grab him by the collar and tell him that was going to breed mediocrity in the organization. Don't hang on to an old method of job evaluation just because that's what you've always done. Do what works best for your organization.

CHAPTER 5

8

A STORY BEHIND EVERY NUMBER

HOW TO COLLECT SALARY DATA

In the last chapter, I gave you an outline of the types of job evaluations and strongly recommended using the market analysis method. Based on that recommendation, I will now give you more detail on how exactly to collect salary data.

INTERNAL ENVIRONMENT

Everyone's internal environment affects their perceptions of job value. It usually goes like this:

Managers typically believe their specialty jobs are paid behind the market (specialty jobs refers to hot jobs that are competitive right now. At the time of this writing, that would be jobs like nurses and data analysts). Managers think they're paid behind the market because those jobs are so hard to hire for and keep. Employees also believe that they're paid too low, because who doesn't think that? It's human nature. Then it's all topped off by recruiters who reach out to those employees and contribute to those perceptions of grandeur because of their own personal agendas. But the buck stops at the top management team, who is constantly trying to reduce labor costs.

Despite all of the complicated politics and perceptions at play, these internal environmental factors don't determine the value of a job. The market does.

WHAT IS THE MARKET?

When we determine the market value of a job, we use precise numbers (even if they are in the form of ranges or guidelines), and people often perceive the market salary for a job as being:

- Definitive.
- Readily measurable.
- A specific number (as in the market average).
- Not open for interpretation.
- Scientific.

I hate to burst your bubble, but market analysis is not a science—it's a blend of art and science. You can't look at the numbers from a market analysis and take it as gospel. It requires some interpretation.

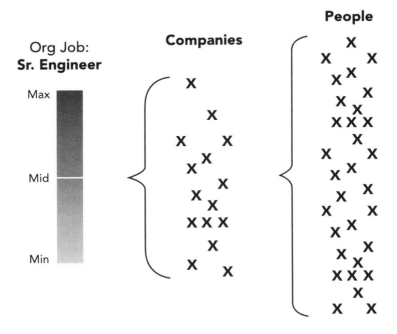

For example, when you get market data, you might get a single average salary number for, say, a senior engineer position. Some companies will pay that position $105,000 a year, some will pay $85,750 a year, and others will pay all over in that range. But the average comes out to $90,000 per year. That doesn't mean that number is set in stone— that's just the average. You have to look at that number and interpret, judge, and use discretion to determine what it means for your organization.

But let's step back for a second. Where do you get that data?

- Market data sources.
- Third-party surveys.
- Off-the-shelf surveys.
- Government data.
- Subscription services.
- Online data.

No matter what type of survey data you use, I implore you not to use informal surveys with your employees and colleagues. It's natural for you to go to people in your industry and ask them, "Hey, what are you paying your senior engineers?" But as soon as you start doing that, it becomes an antitrust violation.

Seriously.

Why? Because it's considered price-fixing and collusion, which is a big freaking deal. In the eyes of the DOL, you could use that information to artificially keep wages low in your industry. So please: don't do an informal survey.

PRICE FIXING IN HEALTHCARE

Entire industries have been brought to task for price-fixing. This happened in the healthcare industry. They held monthly meetings where industry leaders would get together and set salaries for nurses at certain prices, artificially keeping them low.

Even if you're not willfully price-fixing, the government might see it that way, and you'd be in hot water just like the healthcare industry.

YOU HAVE TO PAY TO PLAY

Everyone wants the convenience and value of survey data without giving anything up, but you have to participate in order to get access to the data. Why should you participate in a survey?

- So you can pay employees competitively.
- Adjust your pay based on the market.
- Establish salary ranges in your organization.
- Estimate overall labor costs.
- Analyze data for HR-related projects (such as creating bonus plans).
- Be a good citizen in the HR community.

I run a survey that is free to participate in. I could charge between $5,000 and $7,000 for it, but I see that as an unnecessary barrier to good data collection. Because people don't want to pay for surveys, that leads to less robust data. That could cause people in our industry to crowdsource data themselves in their organization and in their community, which would lead to low-quality data.

It's a tedious process filling out surveys, and it can take hours. The last thing I want to do is make you go through all of that effort and then pay for the privilege to do so. You can participate in our free survey by visiting the CHRG website: chrg.compensationhr.com/surveys.

HOW TO USE SURVEY DATA

The data you collect isn't just salary information. It may also include:

- Policies and practices.
- Prerequisites.
- Benefits.

And you can use that data for all kinds of practical uses. As an HR professional myself, I use data constantly to:

RESOLVE DAILY ISSUES

If an employee comes to you saying they have an added responsibility and need to be paid for it, you can use the data to figure out how much more to pay them, if at all.

MARKET PRICE A SINGLE JOB

If you're hiring for a single job, or you have an employee up for review or promotion in a single position, you can use the data to figure out what salary to pay that single job.

MARKET PRICE THE ENTIRE ORGANIZATION

This is what we set out to do: look at every job in your organization every year and compare your salaries to the market salaries of your competition. You can then match that with your pay philosophy, whether you want to pay above market, below market, or at market (we'll get more into pay philosophy in a moment).

COMPENSATION PLANNING AND BUDGETING

You can use the data to plan your budget for the upcoming years, rather than flying by the seat of your pants each year.

WHAT USING SURVEY DATA CAN DO FOR YOU

- Improve your external competitiveness.
- Attract and retain a productive workforce
- Treat your employees equitably.
- Match your salaries to your pay policies and philosophy.

DEFINING YOUR SURVEY MARKET

Depending on the size of your organization and the level you're acquiring data for, your survey market will change.

GEOGRAPHICAL

As we discussed earlier, different job groups will have different markets: executives may have a national market, professionals may have a regional market, and trade and support roles may have a local market.

For the most part, unless you're hiring a new CEO, you'll look at a commutable distance of about thirty to sixty miles from your business.

WHO ARE YOUR COMPETITORS?

Your competition also defines your survey market. You want to figure out if your competitive organizations are represented in the survey you're using, and if not, you want to find out which one they are using (which you can do by looking at the survey participant list included in the survey). Which leads to the next point...

HOW TO CHOOSE YOUR SURVEY

You'll want to choose your survey based on:

- Jobs, industries, and scope factors covered.
- Job description quality.
- Data quality, sample size, methodology.
- Participants.
- Timing of the report (how recent it is).
- Cost and participant discounts.

JOB MATCHING AND THE 70 PERCENT RULE

Because job matching is so important in survey participation, I want to bring all of this back to the importance of job descriptions. You want to match your organization's benchmark jobs to the survey jobs based on the descriptions you wrote. You don't have to find the perfect match. Just get at least 70 percent of an overlap between the job you're hiring for and the job in the survey data. Because in our world, there's no such thing as a perfect match.

HOW TO MATCH JOBS

- Narrow down potential job matches based on title.
- Read survey job descriptions to determine best match.
- Ask content experts if you're unsure.
  - For example, I struggle matching IT jobs. I can't differentiate between programmers and systems analysts. There are so many combinations that I'll head to the CTO of an organization to help me match one of the job descriptions to the survey

descriptions (which are generic). So you don't have to know everything. Get help when you need it.

- Don't match the same employee to two different jobs.
  - If you have a hybrid job in your organization—such as a role that handles both human resources and payroll—you don't want to match that with a payroll-only job, because your job has a huge HR function, too. My solution? Don't match it at all. When the results are published, you can blend the data from the HR role with the payroll position.
- It's not necessary to match all levels.
  - For example, if the survey has six levels for a specific job, and I only have four, I don't need to force it. Pick the four levels that match the best, and move on.

PAY PHILOSOPHY

What you do with the market data depends on your organization's compensation philosophy. There are basically three choices for pay philosophy:

- Pay below market (lag policy).
- Pay at market (pay relative to competition).
- Pay above market (lead policy).

If you can't afford to pay at market or above market, a good way to find a middle ground is to pay 10 percent below market and offer great benefits. Most people won't feel that 10 percent loss acutely, and with top-tier benefits like health insurance, dental, life insurance, and 401k, they will feel like they more than make up for the lower pay, so they're happy. But you save millions of dollars by doing that, because those benefits don't come close to covering the 10 percent below-market price you've chosen.

In my experience, about 80 percent of organizations want to pay at market, about 10 percent want to pay above market, and another 10 percent want to pay below market.

You might automatically say you want to pay above market, but there are a lot of hidden costs associated with that philosophy. You might be able to retain high-quality employees, but you'll have to offer your products at a higher price to compensate for the difference. The converse goes for a lag policy: if you want to pay below market, you have to be willing to accept higher turnover, lower-skilled employees, and a business predicated on high-volume sales.

You have to find a balance. If you have a lead policy and crap products, you'll go out of business.

LEAD TOO MUCH, AND IT'LL LEAD TO BANKRUPTCY

I had a client who had to hire three hundred people to sell his company's tech product—some router widget. They had venture capitalist funding, so he felt they had to hire right away. Now, their philosophy was to pay above market, but they had no idea how much above market.

When they got ahold of me, they'd been in operation for a year, and they struggled to hang on to people they recruited.

"We want to do a market analysis. I think our compensation might be a bit high."

Well, I ran the analysis, and you know what we found? Every single job was at least 30 percent above market. I'd never seen anything like it before. To sustain those kinds of labor costs, especially for new hires, you have to sell really expensive products. This widget was not expensive enough to rationalize it.

When I told the CEO what I'd found, he started crying. He knew that this meant doom.

His philosophy was to pay above market, but if you don't know what the market is, you're just throwing darts at the board. They paid above market because they needed to get more than three hundred people in a matter of months, but it shot them in the foot. To compensate for those wild compensation levels, they had to price their product too high. Within six months of me working with them, they went out of business.

Their example underscores the importance of not only managing labor costs but also realizing that having a pay philosophy doesn't make a difference if you don't know what the market is. That's like trying to buy stocks when you don't know what the stock price is. You might as well go to the casino at that point.

WHY IS PAY PHILOSOPHY IMPORTANT?

Aside from being required for some companies, for you it will guide your decisions. Your pay philosophy will determine which data points you use, such as central tendency (simple average, weighted average, or median) and percentile, and how you trend the data, such as aging (we'll talk more about aging data in a moment).

For example, if your philosophy is to match the market, you will use simple averages, medians, or weighted averages for your jobs' salaries. If your philosophy is to lag or lead the market, you'll look at percentiles. If your philosophy is to lead the market, you'll look at, say, the 75th percentile of the salaries, and if your philosophy is to lag the market, you might look at the 25th percentile of salaries for your positions.

HOW TO AGE SURVEY DATA

The other reason a pay philosophy is important is because it helps you age the data. Now, this is a somewhat convoluted concept, so follow me closely here.

Here's a good example to illustrate what aging data is, why it's important, and how to do it:

The data from the survey I run is effective on March 1 of every year. We ask all of our participants to tell us what their salaries were on that date. But it takes time to compile that data, so we usually publish the survey at the end of May. Therefore, when you first look at the survey data, it's already several months old. The compensation market moves every day—people get promotions, pay raises, and so on every day of the week. What's more, let's say you receive the survey in May, but you don't need to use it until September. By then, it's half a year old.

In order to "update" that data to fit the current salaries, you have to age it. How do you determine how much to "age" it by?

MARKET MOVEMENT

To effectively age data, you'll want to determine two aspects of market movement:

Projected Movement—this is based on the salary surveys. For instance, your survey will ask participants what their salary increases will be for this year and next year. This allows us to project salary movement in the future.

Historical Movement—this is based on year-to-year increases in salary in the past.

The aging rate may vary based on:

- Job levels.
- Industry.
- Geography.

- Compensation components (such as base and total compensation).

Using both of these movement rates and those other factors, we determine that salaries for any given position will increase X percent in the next year.

For example, let's say your survey determines that data analyst salaries will increase by 3 percent in the next year.

You start by dividing that number by 12, and you get 0.25. That's the amount the salary will increase every month. So, again, if the data was collected for March 1 and you start using it in September, you need to age the data by:

0.25 x 6 months = 1.5 (meaning your salary data will increase by 1.5 percent over the course of 6 months).

Let's say the average data analyst salary is $60,000 in the survey. You now have all of the information you need to age the data: $60,000 x 1.015 = **$60,900.**

If you work in a large organization, that aging makes a huge difference—not only in your employees' lives but also to your bottom line. And most people don't know about this, let alone do it. Most organizations just look at the survey results without looking at the trend data. If you don't age the data, you're doing a disservice to your employees. You can set yourself apart from your competition by aging your data and paying fairly.

COMPENSATION CALCULATIONS

If you want to compare your organization's pay to the survey rate for a job, use the following formula:

Your Company's Average Salary Rate / Survey Rate. The Market Ratio would be the resulting number times 100.

If that number comes out to 100 percent, you're paying at market.

The second calculation will tell you the adjustment percentage, as in the percent increase required to match the market:

(Survey Rate – Your Company Average) / Your Company Average = Adjustment Rate

And just so you know, here's an example of what a salary survey might look like:

Base Compensation

Level	Org Wtd Avg	Inc Wtd Avg	Inc 25th %ile	Inc 50th %ile	Inc 75th %ile
M4	97.3	97.3	94.5	97.5	100.2
M3	82.0	81.9	77.8	80.9	84.0
M2	69.3	69.6	65.1	69.1	73.6
M1	57.0	59.1	54.0	58.1	62.1
S5	63.6	62.9	59.6	63.0	67.5
S4	55.4	55.6	53.9	55.6	57.5
S3	50.4	50.5	48.7	51.0	52.5
S2	45.2	45.0	42.9	44.9	46.9
S1	38.6	39.1	35.5	38.1	41.9

Variable Compensation

Level	Average Target %	Average Actual $
M4	15.0	14.7
M3	10.0	8.4
M2	9.0	6.1
M1	0.0	3.0
S5	5.0	2.6
S4	4.0	2.1
S3	5.9	2.8
S2	7.1	2.8
S1	4.5	1.6

Total Compensation

Level	Org Wtd Avg	Inc Wtd Avg	Inc 25th %ile	Inc 50th %ile	Inc 75th %ile
M4	102.1	102.1	96.0	100.2	108.0
M3	85.6	86.1	81.5	84.5	89.4
M2	71.5	71.4	66.0	73.4	74.8
M1	57.4	59.4	54.0	59.1	62.4
S5	64.3	63.6	60.3	63.0	69.5
S4	56.1	56.2	53.9	56.5	58.5
S3	51.0	51.4	48.9	51.5	54.0
S2	45.8	45.7	43.3	45.3	48.1
S1	38.9	39.2	35.5	38.2	42.1

A STORY BEHIND EVERY NUMBER

These formulas might be helpful, but this stuff is not pure

science or only math. Compensation, as I've said before, is a blend of art and science. Regardless of your company's philosophy, you want to examine the data closely and interpret it using your skills and judgment to make sure you're making the most out of your company's biggest expense. You want to be accurate, but you don't want to be so stubborn and surgically precise that it negatively affects your data and your employees.

When you step back and look at everything, you'll see that some of your job matches and other assumptions weren't accurate. It happens to every compensation expert. If you see one of your jobs is way off the mark from the market average, it's possible that your company is underpaying for that role, but use your analytical skills to determine if you just mismatched the job description.

You're not a robot, and compensation is not a computer operation. Don't let the data blind you to common sense. There's a story behind every number, and blending that story with the science of the data is how you find harmony between the art and science of compensation.

I've made a strong recommendation that you use market analysis, and we've gone through how to use market data to determine the average salaries for your organization's jobs. Now, in the next chapter, we'll use that information to develop your compensation program.

CHAPTER 6

8

SPREADING THE WEALTH

HOW TO DEVELOP A COMPENSATION PROGRAM

In this chapter, you'll learn how to design your compensation program. You'll do that by developing your pay policy trend line and comparing that to what the market is paying versus what you're paying.

As part of this process, you'll determine the salary ranges for your jobs, how many levels each job has, and what determines movement between levels.

YOU CAN'T JUST CHANGE THE MIDPOINT

Sometimes a company will contact me and tell me that they can't keep any employees. One of my first requests is to see their salary ranges for the position.

Based on those ranges, I'll run a quick and simple calculation: I'll calculate the width between the salary minimum and the maximum, then determine the midpoint based on those numbers. Then I'll compare that to how their salary levels are designed at the moment to see if there's any underlying logic to the different levels of compensation within the job. Nine times out of ten, there is absolutely no rhyme or reason—these salary ranges may as well have been drawn up on a napkin.

That's how I know I can help a client. Because the name of the game for your compensation program is:

CONSISTENCY

You determine your pay rates based on a number of factors:

- Kinds/levels of required knowledge and skills.
- Type of business.
- Size of your business.
- Your management philosophy.
- Your geographic location.
- Profitability.
- Employee performance.
- Turnover rates.
- Union status.
- Supply and demand of labor.

PAY POLICY LINE

As I said, your goal in this chapter is to determine what I call the pay policy line. Here's how you do that:

Let's say we're looking at your customer service position, and it has four levels of advancement from entry-level to senior. You'll group the salary ranges for each level together and find the midpoint in the salary range for each level. That midpoint, ideally, will be the market rate for that position at that level. If someone is getting paid below that midpoint, they're paid below market, and if they're paid above that midpoint, they're paid above market.

You manage your offers to new candidates, promotions, and everything in between by using that midpoint as your guiding light. Therefore, because each level of an individual job will be paid less than the next level, if you draw a line between your midpoints for a job from level one to level four, that line will angle upwards. That's your pay policy line, which goes through the midpoint of every level of a job.

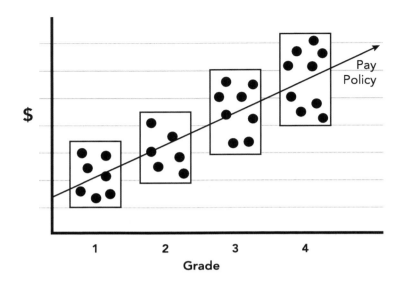

Every level of every job has a minimum, a maximum, and a midpoint between those two.

DETERMINING RANGE SPREAD

Now, you want to make sure there's no funny business going on and that your midpoint is actually in the middle of your salary range. I've had people contact me who want to change their midpoints but not increase the minimum or maximum rates.

It doesn't work like that. Instead, I start by walking them through how to figure out their salary range spread.

Let's say for one job level, your minimum salary is $50,000

and your maximum is \$75,000. That means your salary range spread is 50 percent because the difference between the minimum and the maximum is 50 percent, and the midpoint is \$62,500.

(Maximum – Minimum) / (Minimum) = Spread Percentage

(75,000 - 50,000) / 50,000 = 25,000 / 50,000 = .5 = 50%

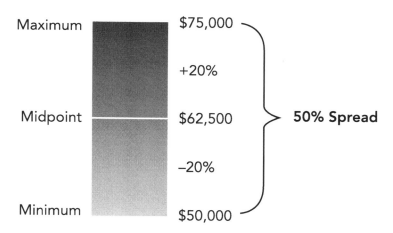

I don't want you to get too bogged down with this math; I just want you to understand the basics. The point is, you can't just anchor the minimum and hope to artificially keep your midpoint low, so you can pay people below market under the guise of paying market rates. You have to update these numbers every year for this very reason. As market rates increase, you have to increase all three numbers: your minimum, your maximum, and your midpoint.

Your goal is to make sure that you have enough overlap between job levels so that when an employee gets promoted, their salary will be positioned correctly in the new salary range.

TYPICAL RANGE SPREADS

- Administrative positions 40 percent.
- Professional and supervisor positions 50 percent.
- Managerial and executive positions 60+ percent.

As you can see, the higher up the hierarchy, the higher the spreads. The most important thing is that you want to offer more growth opportunities as people advance, which is why the salary ranges increase as you climb the internal hierarchy.

WHAT IS A COMPA-RATIO AND HOW DO YOU CALCULATE IT?

In chapter 5, I talked about the market ratio, as in how well your internal pay compares to the market rate. Now I want to explain something called the compa-ratio, which is the relationship of your actual pay to the midpoint of a specific job at a specific level.

Let's say your current salary for a mid-level administrative position is $60,000, and you've determined that the midpoint for that job at that level is $62,500 (because the maximum is $75,000 and the minimum is $50,000).

You use the following formula to determine the compa-ratio:

Current Salary / Midpoint for that Level = Compa-ratio

So: $60,000 / $62,500 = .96 = **96%**

If your philosophy is to pay at market, your goal is usually to have the overall organizational compa-ratio be 100 percent, meaning, on average, the actual salaries are at the midpoint.

My rule of thumb: if you see any job that has a compa-ratio that's below 90 percent or above 110 percent, it requires a second look. Anything in between that range is in good shape.

EFFECTIVE PERIOD

As you determine your compensation program, you have to determine when and how people are given salary increases. The effective period is when employee increases take effect. There are three different options:

- **Fixed focal point**—means all increases for all employees are effective at the same time. Some organizations choose this option because it's predictable, and you know exactly what your budget will be for the salary increases.
- **Anniversary date**—means your employees get increases based on their date of hire or job entry. This staggers the increases throughout the year, which may be easier to handle in terms of cash flow rather than triggering them all at once.
- **Variable timing**—means employees get increases based on performance, which is less predictable but highly recommended.

ADMINISTRATIVE CONSIDERATIONS

ATTRACTING WORKERS IN SHORT SUPPLY

What I see in a lot of organizations is that they have a pay philosophy to match the market, but when it comes to jobs that are in short supply (such as software developers at the time of this writing), they change their pay philosophy to lead the market. It may make sense for certain positions at certain times, but make sure you do this consciously and not out of desperation.

PAY COMPRESSION

This is when you hire someone externally for more than what you're paying someone already in that position. For example, if you have an internal person making $50,000 a year in a job, and you hire someone externally for the same job at the same level and pay them $55,000 a year, you may upset your current employee, even if that's what you had to do to get that outside talent.

EMPLOYEES PAID AT MAXIMUM

Personally, I don't think it's ever a good idea to pay employees at the top of a salary range. At that point, you should consider freezing the salary and providing lump-sum increases.

WHAT'S NEXT?

Now that you've designed your compensation program by determining salary ranges for each job, how many levels each job has, and what determines a promotion, it's time to conduct performance evaluations.

CHAPTER 7

8

HOW ARE EMPLOYEES DOING?

HOW TO CONDUCT EFFECTIVE PERFORMANCE EVALUATIONS

In chapter 6, I guided you through developing your compensation program, including figuring out your salary ranges and midpoints. In this chapter, I'll teach you how to conduct effective performance evaluations, which you'll use to determine where in your salary ranges your employees should be compensated.

You can call this process by any number of names that are all interchangeable:

- Performance management.
- Performance evaluations.
- Performance appraisal.
- Performance review.

In short, performance management is the act of observing, identifying, and measuring human behavior in your organization. You will use it as a key tool to make sure you get your desired business results by rewarding behavior that reinforces your company's core values. It will ideally measure everyone against the same values, so consistency is key to performance management.

Furthermore, performance evaluations should:

- Be a continuous process (employees don't like to be surprised, so you don't want this to feel like they're being singled out).
- Be a chance to discuss the employee's work, performance, and career goals.
- Address both behavior and outcomes.
- Establish specific goals and measurements.
- Measure the employee's contributions.
- Identify career objectives and development plans.

When done well, performance evaluations have massive benefits to employees, their supervisors, and the organization at large.

THE 4X4 PERFORMANCE MANAGEMENT PROCESS

Here's a simple guideline to perform performance reviews. It's based on having a meeting between an employee and manager four times per year, consisting of four questions:

Question 1: What accomplishments have you had since the last time we met?

Question 2: What are the most important things you will accomplish before our next meeting?

Question 3: What challenges are you facing today?

Question 4: How can I help you be your best?

You have a conversation every quarter, the employee recaps the meeting, the manager reviews and approves the responses, and the employee finalizes by archiving the report.

Some benefits of the 4x4 review process:

- Increase in employee/manager communication.
- Increase in employee engagement in the workplace.
- Employees look forward to the conversations and receiving feedback from managers.
- Managers look forward to the process because it is simple and easy to complete.
- 100 percent participation.

BENEFITS OF PERFORMANCE EVALUATIONS

FOR THE EMPLOYEE

- Knows what is expected and how performance will be judged.
- Can evaluate own progress and effectiveness.
- Can effectively plan work time.
- Understands the criteria for being rewarded/promoted.

- Is motivated to continually develop.
- Can discuss career development.

FOR THE SUPERVISOR

- Clearly expresses expectations and priorities.
- Maintains good communication with employees.
- Helps identify training and development needs.
- Motivates employees using formal recognition.
- Obtains improved performance from employees.
- Can maintain ongoing communication.

FOR THE ORGANIZATION

- The individual employee objectives dovetail together with organization goals.
- Can plan and budget more effectively.
- Has more motivated and productive employees.
- Stays competitive by dealing with non-performance.
- Avoids employee relations and legal problems.

As you can see, this is an incredibly valuable and important process for any organization, all the way through your ranks.

HOW PERFORMANCE REVIEWS REINFORCE YOUR CORE VALUES

Let's say one of your core values is that the customer comes first. You'll want to make sure you have an objective around customer service that's measured in every performance review. For example, you could create an objective that people answering calls must answer within three rings and answer in a pleasant and helpful way. That way, they know exactly what's expected of them, and you know they're behaving in a way that reinforces your core values.

WHY DO SOME PERFORMANCE EVALUATION SYSTEMS FAIL?

I know it's an odd way to look at it—focusing on why they fail as opposed to why they succeed—but I focus on failure here because so many performance evaluations do go wrong, so we need to make corrections so yours work as intended.

REARVIEW MIRROR STRATEGY

This is a huge reason why employees don't like performance evaluations: because they tend to focus on the past and critique behavior rather than improve it. It leads to them feeling like victims, as though the evaluation is being done to them, rather than feeling like a partner in the process.

TOO INFREQUENT

Again, you want to make sure it's a continuous process, not a once-a-year formality that looks at the past and focuses on what the employee messed up. It should be a positive, constructive, and consistent meeting.

TOO FINELY-TUNED RATING SYSTEM

This means there are too many degrees to how employees are rated. I have one client who has five levels of ratings, but there's a plus and minus for every level. So really, there are fifteen different ratings, which confuses people. They don't know why they get a 3- as opposed to a 3+. Keep it simple.

INCONSISTENCIES

Sometimes, I see rating inflation where managers rate everybody as outstanding, a perfect five out of five, and handsome to boot. But the truth is, there should be a curve of performance: some people should be below average, some average, and some above average.

NOT CONNECTED TO BUSINESS GOALS

Without clear and identifiable objectives for the factors being rated, people feel as though the evaluation is arbitrary. And in most cases, they are totally correct. Connect every factor of being evaluated to a business goal, and there will be a clear *why* behind every evaluation.

FOCUSED ON BEHAVIOR, NOT RESULTS

People don't like feeling policed or micromanaged. They want to be left alone to do their work and for you to see the results. If your performance evaluations focus on behavior over results, you'll get a lot of people who want to *appear* to do good work rather than actually do good work.

THE REST...

Beyond these common reasons for failure, there plenty of other reasons why performance evaluations fail:

- Lack of discussion of personal and career development.
- Focused on recent or short-term results.
- Not linked to your organization's rewards systems (which we'll discuss in chapters 9 and 10).
- Poorly prepared supervisors.
- Lack of participation or support from top management.
- Lack of participation of users in developing the process.
- Managers' lack of time to do a quality job.
- The process is too complicated or time-consuming.

One common way people make this process too complicated

is by having overly complex forms with seven or eight pages worth of factors being rated. It's completely unnecessary.

Having said that, what is the right approach to create a successful evaluation system?

HOW TO CREATE A SUCCESSFUL PERFORMANCE EVALUATION SYSTEM

First, make sure your evaluation forms are streamlined and simple, and for god's sake make them electronic, not hard copies! Beyond that, there is no one-size-fits-all evaluation form; you just want to make sure the end product is:

- Relevant.
- Helpful.
- Easily understood.
- Accepted by both the employees and the supervisors.
- Not overly complex.
- User-friendly.

Aside from those basic principles to create a high-quality performance evaluation system, make sure you have some standards represented throughout the process.

Use ongoing performance criteria—these criteria will be based on job content as described in the employee's job description (which is just another reason why it's so important to have documented and frequently updated job descriptions).

Done on a job-by-job basis—you want to customize the evaluation format to every person so they know exactly what's expected of them. It's time-consuming and labor-intensive to do it this way, and it requires detailed and thorough job analysis, but doing it this way promotes a clear understanding of expectations in each job. That will save you money in the long run as your employees are less likely to do redundant work and more likely to be focused on clear objectives.

These objective standards that you're evaluating should also reflect a certain set of other characteristics:

- They are based on the job, not the person.
- They are achievable.
- They are understood.
- They are agreed upon.
- They are as specific and measurable as possible.
- They are time-oriented.
- They are written.
- They are subject to change.

GOAL SETTING

You can choose to approach your evaluations by using

hard goals as a strong indicator of performance. Using this framework, you would sit down with your employees to develop specific accomplishments that they plan to complete within a given time frame. These goals have to be:

- Mutually agreed upon.
- Specific.
- Measurable.
- Time-bound.
- Challenging.

Because they'll be created in collaboration with the employee, the objectives will vary, even for individuals on the same job. Once those goals are reached, new goals can be established, which creates a highly-motivated and successful workforce.

The end results of the goals should be predictable, and the results should be quantifiable and cumulative. They should also be understood and agreed upon by the employee, supervisor, and the organization. This goal-setting system will only work if the internal and external environments in the company are stable. For example, this will be much harder to accomplish in a fast-changing startup environment or during a major economic downturn.

WHAT DO GOOD GOALS LOOK LIKE?

You can determine key business results with managers for the whole organization, and from there, look at what operations, systems, and procedures improvements can be made to attain those results. You can also identify innovative activities that would be beneficial to the organization and tie those into goal objectives.

And don't forget about employees' personal development, which is incredibly valuable and important to them.

Let's take an accountant, for example, since every organization likely has one. Some good goals for an accountant might be:

· Implement a new accounting system.
· Participate in payroll software demos.
· Transition to a new payroll system.

How many objectives should you have in your goal setting? Three to five is the best number. Anything above that gets too complicated, and anything below that isn't challenging enough. The number you choose in the end will depend on the amount of time available to pursue the objectives and how complex they are.

In short, I think this specific goal-setting framework is a very positive way to frame your performance evaluations.

CHECKLISTS

Another potential element of performance evaluations is a checklist. I love checklists. They're simple, clear, and direct. They are widely used in performance evaluations because they're easy to complete, and they evaluate employee performance based on established factors.

They're often used for hourly production and other nonexempt employees, and they're great in that context, but even I'm not convinced that they're valuable for performance improvement. They often focus too much on employee traits rather than observable behaviors and results. And people who fill out checklist evaluations often see them as a distant, necessary bureaucratic evil as opposed to a tool for collaboration between the employee, the supervisor, and the organization. However, I do believe that they're useful as a supplement to other, more robust elements of a successful performance evaluation system.

SOME DESIGN CONSIDERATIONS FOR CHECKLISTS

- **Decide if all factors are of equal importance—**depending on your organization's goals, you may want to weigh certain factors (such as customer service) as more important than others.
- **Make factors as relevant as possible—**if someone is only working on the production floor and never inter-

acting with customers, it doesn't do much good to ask them a bunch of customer service questions on a checklist.

- **Limit factors to a reasonable number**—the best range here is between six and twelve.
- **Set standards**—you need to have a standard for each factor in each position; otherwise, you'll ask people questions, they'll give you responses, but you'll have nothing to compare them to.

NARRATIVES

The narrative framework is the exact opposite of the checklist. In short, a narrative-based performance evaluation asks the manager to write a couple of paragraphs about their employee's performance.

Personally, I see this as a useful addition to other evaluation frameworks—as a solo framework, it leaves a lot to be desired. It can be very subjective, and it's heavily dependent on the writing skills of the appraiser. As such, there is a major lack of consistency when you ask for narrative reviews.

SOME DEFUNCT EVALUATION SYSTEMS
EMPLOYEE COMPARISON/RANKING

This is an old-school evaluation system that major corporations like GE, Microsoft, Hewlett-Packard, and others used at one point but have abandoned over time. It consists of ranking employees from best to worst on a basis of overall performance or factor-specific performance. It's really easy to use ranking to compare people at the extremes, such as the top performers and the lowest-level performers, but it's incredibly difficult to make it work in the middle.

FORCED DISTRIBUTION

Because these companies struggled to rank their mid-level employees, they started to move to a forced distribution model. This is where they forced a bell curve of a small number of low performers, a high number of average performers, and a small number of high performers.

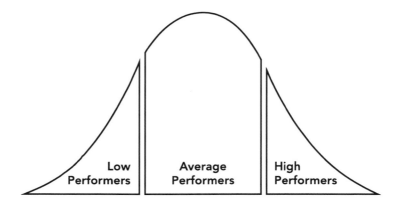

This seems to make sense on paper, but it had some terrible unforeseen consequences in practice. For one, in organizations where there weren't as many below-average performers as the bell curve required, supervisors were compelled to rate some employees as below-average unnecessarily, just to reach the quota of the bell curve. What happened then is that these corporations constantly overturned the bottom 10 percent of performers, and had to rehire and rerank new hires as they came in.

This created tense, cutthroat environments. I know because I worked in one of these environments back in the day at Hewlett-Packard. The forced distribution created a lot of competition because employees knew they were being ranked, so to avoid finding themselves on the chopping block, they'd set out to sabotage other employees any way they could.

Not to mention you have to have at least thirty-five to fifty employees to make this system statistically viable (even if it's still morally bankrupt), and most companies don't have departments that size.

I'm telling you, this system creates an environment like something out of *Wall Street*. Every year, the managers would go into a room with no windows, put each employee up on the screen, and ask the supervisor to explain what the employee had done that year and where they ranked in the distribution. So right off the bat, there was a bias because the supervisor inevitably wanted to defend their department's employees. They'd do anything to force someone else's employees to get on the chopping block, which led to fighting even within these manager meetings (which they called "calibration meetings"). What's worse is that if an employee found out they were ranked low, they'd blame the manager for not fighting hard enough for them.

It was a nasty environment, and I'm glad people don't use this ranking system anymore. When CEOs ask me about it because they hear GE used it once upon a time, I tell them that story, and they drop the idea very quickly.

RATINGS SCALES

So this all begs the question of how you quantify the data your employees are giving you. The answer is ratings scales. For example, for every factor you ask your employees about, we suggest you have a scale of three to five responses available (research shows that supervisors can discriminate between five to seven performance levels, so you don't want to push that capacity).

Sample ratings are:

- Developing.
- Meets expectations.
- Exceeds expectations.
- Outstanding.

There is some debate as to whether an odd or even number of ratings is ideal. The best advice is that you need to have some consistency throughout to fight against rating inflation. It's easy for people to start saying that everyone and everything is outstanding, and that's not helpful. You must have checks and balances in place.

WHO SHOULD FILL OUT EVALUATION FORMS?

The same way you can choose a combination of checklists and narrative evaluation forms, you can choose a combination of who fills out those forms.

SELF-APPRAISAL

Self-appraisal is always illustrative, and it's the most frequently used approach. It enhances communication between supervisors and employees because they answer the same questions about the employee and they can discuss discrepancies they find. For a self-appraisal, you can ask questions such as:

- What critical skills and abilities does my job require? To what extent do I feel I have the skills and knowledge I need to succeed on the job?
- What do I like best about my job? Least?
- What were my accomplishments during this review period?

- What goals or standards did I fall short of achieving?
- What have I done since my last appraisal to prepare myself for more responsibility?
- Is there anything about the organization that hinders my effectiveness?
- What changes would improve my performance?
- Does my present job make the best use of my capabilities? How could I become more productive?
- Do I thoroughly understand my role, responsibilities, and accountabilities?
- What new goals and standards should be established for the next appraisal period? Which old ones need to be modified or deleted?

PEER REVIEW

Peer appraisal offers a lot more challenges, both ethically and regarding accuracy, but they can be helpful. This is a process by which people in a specific department or team evaluate each other. Typically it's anonymous, and the input goes through the manager. This approach does not work in a cutthroat environment—it requires trust (for example, it wouldn't work in an employee ranking system because everyone would just wind up trashing each other). It can take a couple of different forms:

- 100 percent participation from peer groups on a regularly-scheduled basis.

- Getting input from team members, then having a third-party review and summarize each person's data to convey to the team.

Now, if you think about it, doing peer evaluation for even a ten-person team would be incredibly time-consuming. Ten people being asked to rate nine other people is a lot of feedback and a lot of work. It might provide another good data point, and it can improve communication and leadership on the team, but it risks breeding distrust and can deteriorate a team quickly. Peer reviews should not be the sole basis of your evaluation system, only an optional supplement.

EMPLOYEE-SUPERVISOR FEEDBACK

These can offer some incredible insight, but many managers and supervisors don't want to subject themselves to this often-humbling process. I would say less than 10 percent of organizations ask employees to fill out evaluations of their supervisors, and when they do, they often use it as a development tool just to train the manager. But I think they're a great tool, especially if the manager is open-minded and they have a lot of guts. Leaving it up to managers to get that feedback of their own volition usually yields nothing. I think feedback should be a two-way street. Some guidelines for employee-supervisor evaluations:

- Keep them anonymous (by making the evaluation consist of at least four responses).
- Assure employees that there is no threat of retaliation.
- Only human resources or a third-party sees raw data.
- Manager sees summary results only.

TIMING

With employee evaluations, you have to consider the timing. People expect some kind of pay increase to accompany their evaluation. Some research says your employee reviews should be done separately from when you decide salary increases; that way you can all focus on the performance first, then wait a few weeks or months before having the compensation conversation. I don't agree with that. I think salary and performance reviews should be tied together.

End the review by thanking the employee for their hard work, and transition into the reward conversation. That's when you show them where their new salary fits in the salary range, and they know there's concrete justification for their salary and what they can do to improve it (we'll discuss this more in the next chapter).

The only way to screw any of this up is to have a poorly-defined performance appraisal system. Without employee evaluations, you leave yourself open to wrongful discharge and discrimination cases.

HOW TO AVOID LEGAL PITFALLS IN PERFORMANCE EVALUATIONS

Here are some common assessment mistakes managers make that leave you and your whole organization open to legal ramifications:

- Prejudice and personal bias.
- The halo or horn effect—meaning the manager assumes a certain employee can do no wrong or can do no right.
- Recency effect—this is a very common phenomenon, where employees step up their performance a few months before the evaluation date so the manager only remembers what good they've done lately.
- Leniency error—this is when a manager rates everyone really highly regardless of performance.
- Central tendency—this is the tendency to rate everyone as satisfactory, average, or meeting expectations so they don't differentiate.
- Lack of connection between appraisal and pay.

The point is, your managers need to be aware of these common errors because they can impact people's salaries and impact your company's future.

Incorrect performance assessments, as a result of these common errors, lead to incorrect rewards, which lead to incorrect terminations, which lead to lawsuits.

HOW AND WHEN TO DO THE EVALUATION

Performance evaluation administration is an often overlooked but very important aspect of performance management. I've found that if I just leave it up to managers to do it, they don't do it on time, which means we don't give people their salary increases on time. One of the most discouraging things for employees to experience is when they get their pay increase late. As such, you have to:

- Decide whether to administer evaluations on a common review date or on the employee's job anniversary date.
- Distribute reports that capture on-time performance evaluation delivery.
- Charge managers' budgets as a punishment for late performance reviews (you can do this by charging their budget for the cost of retroactive pay increases).
- Decide whether to use merit matrix guidelines, which we will review in chapter 8.

Now that you've developed a performance evaluation system, I'm going to teach you how to take that data and use it to determine rewards for employees.

8

PAY FOR PERFORMANCE

HOW TO DEVELOP A PERFORMANCE-BASED COMPENSATION PROGRAM

The best thing you can do for your employees is to link their pay to their performance. In this chapter, I'm going to teach you how to properly pay your employees based on the data we've gathered so far.

The thing is, about 80 percent of organizations say they pay for performance, but most of the time, that's not true—they don't truly link performance with rewards. There are multiple reasons why this may be the case:

- Managers find it hard to give low ratings.
- Appraisal methods used can make the evaluation of performance difficult.

- Cost restraints can prohibit high rewards.
- Gap in time between the appraisal and pay rewards diminish the motivation link.
- Employee perceptions between expected and actual rewards may not match.
- Emphasis on individual and not team performance can break down teamwork.

MEASURING AND PAYING FOR PERFORMANCE

Overall, you want to ensure the evaluations in chapter 7 were done objectively. That's why I recommend employees have access to an appeal system, whereby they can appeal to the next level manager if they don't see eye to eye on their evaluation. It's also important to communicate your organization's pay policy and the process you use to determine pay increases so everyone is on the same page.

As we compare their performance to the salary range minimums, maximums, and midranges you calculated earlier, you can see how people should be paid relative to their performance.

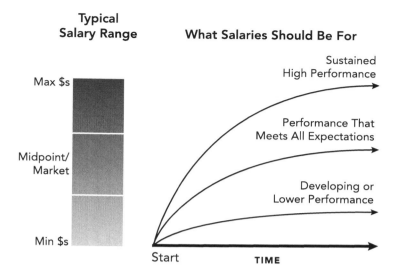

Typical Salary Range

Max $s

Midpoint/ Market

Min $s

What Salaries Should Be For

Sustained High Performance

Performance That Meets All Expectations

Developing or Lower Performance

Start

TIME

If someone is still developing or has a lower performance level, their salary will be below the midpoint at their job level. If their performance meets expectations, they will be compensated around the midpoint, and if they sustain high performance, they will slowly inch up to the salary range maximum before moving up to the next level of their job.

NO SUCH THING AS INSTANT EQUITY

As far as the timeline goes, people have to be reasonable. If you hire someone today and realize they're a high-performer next week, they're not going to get a 30 percent increase next month. There is no instant equity. They have to get that pay growth over time. But you also can't wait ten years, either. You have to see them maintain their performance for a sustainable period of time before you can truly make an objective decision on their pay.

Without a formal pay system, there's a good chance you'll inadvertently treat your employees unfairly. The people who give the greatest results should get the greatest rewards, and the people who give the lowest results should get the lowest rewards.

MERIT INCREASE GUIDELINES

Performance Rating

Position In Range	Outstanding	Consistently Exceeds Requirements	Meets Requirements	Developing Toward Meeting Requirements
4th Quartile	3-5%	0-3%	0%	0%
3rd Quartile	5-7%	3-5%	0-3%	0%
2nd Quartile	7-9%	5-7%	3-5%	0-3%
1st Quartile	9-11%	7-9%	5-7%	3-5%

This is a guideline to help you figure out what percentage increases you should be delivering to employees (this framework is based on a standard 4 percent annual salary increase budget). Those quartiles in the "Position in Range" column are where the person sits in the salary range, and that line between the second and third quartiles is the midpoint in the salary range. If you identify where in the salary range someone is being compensated and compare it to their performance rating (outstanding, consistently exceeds requirements, meets requirements, developing toward meeting requirements), you can see what their salary increase should be, if anything.

For example, someone who's already being compensated in the upper quartile of the salary range and is meeting requirements doesn't get a salary increase because they're already maxed out on that range and aren't showing that they're ready to move up. But someone who is meeting requirements and is in the second quartile should be moved up to reflect that they are no longer developing toward meeting requirements.

This is what I call a merit increase matrix process, and it is a great guideline to determine salary percentage increases. The only way you're able to afford those eye-popping increases in the bottom left is to take from what would have been standard increases in the top right, where people are performing below their pay level.

Think about it: those people at the fourth quartile who are meeting requirements are already being paid above market rate, and they are performing at that level—they don't need a pay increase. It's better to put that investment in people who are climbing up the ranks. A lot of people feel bad for the people in the fourth quartile who meet requirements and don't get an increase. Don't feel bad for them. They're already being paid at a premium above market rate—they're not going anywhere.

This is important stuff because if you make these decisions from your emotions instead of from a math standpoint (like we use in this guideline), you'll allocate your resources in the wrong places, and you'll lose really good people. Everything we've talked about has led to this. We did job analyses, we wrote job descriptions, we created the internal hierarchy, we built salary ranges, and we developed a performance management system so we could pay people for their performance, all in alignment.

If any of those elements were done incorrectly, this is where you would see the malfunctions pop up.

CHAPTER 9

MAKING IT COUNT

HOW TO RECOGNIZE AND REWARD EMPLOYEES

I've given you a framework to accurately connect employee pay with their performance and results. Now I'm going to give you ideas for how to recognize and reward your employees outside of their base compensation.

I have to tell you: this part is incredibly important to employees, and too many companies overlook it. People love being recognized for their hard work, and for whatever reason, managers find it hard to do this on a consistent basis. I don't understand it. I am constantly pushing people to recognize and reward their employees with extra recognition.

In this chapter, I'll provide you with ideas for:

- Informal awards.
- No-cost recognition.
- Low-cost rewards.
- Rewarding good work.
- Merchandise rewards.
- Celebrations.
- Employee awards.
- Formal awards.

You don't have to implement everything I set out in this chapter—in fact, it would likely be too much if you did—I always recommend a budget of 0.5-1 percent of payroll dedicated to recognition and rewards. I just want to give you a toolbox to work from.

THE IMPORTANCE OF SINCERITY

Your employees know if you're not sincere with your rewards and recognition. They can feel it. I have some clients who recognize someone on their team at least once a week, and it feels genuine because the employees know they earned it, and they're proud of that.

If you're only doing these things because you feel compelled to, not because anyone actually did anything worth rewarding, people will pick up on that, and it will cause more ill will than if you just did nothing at all. Pay is the most important thing to people in their jobs, no question about it. But this is incredibly important, too, and my goal is for you to realize how important recognition is.

So keep it sincere, keep it authentic, and keep it genuine.

IF YOU DON'T RECOGNIZE YOUR EMPLOYEES, THEY'LL TURN BITTER

I recommend that you do some of these things every week with people. If employees aren't recognized outside of their base compensation, it can turn bad. One client I had only recognized their employees in the monthly meeting minutes during their management meetings when employees weren't present. Then, when the minutes were distributed to the employees, everybody would ignore the actual meeting notes and go straight to the bottom to see if their names were mentioned in the recognition section. The meetings were full of necessary business information, but everyone would skip that just to find their names. This led to bitterness. They'd think, "I wasn't recognized again? This is BS." They developed theories that certain people were favorites, and that led to them never being recognized.

We were at risk of creating a cutthroat environment, so we set up a system where managers would, at the end of every week, tell the CEO who they wanted to recognize, then the CEO would personally recognize those employees. This was a huge motivator for people. But more importantly, it required a shift in thinking from the management team. Many management teams don't want to praise people for doing what's part of their job. However, if you don't, people do their job and never feel like their efforts are seen.

You don't have to only praise people for doing things beyond the scope of their job. You can absolutely recognize them for the daily duties that they do exceptionally.

Making this small change completely turned around the morale of the employees and shifted the mindsets of the managers. It created a more productive, happy environment, and that shift is within your grasp if you make some of these changes, too.

INFORMAL REWARDS

You don't have to do anything over the top with informal rewards. That company had a formalized system, but their method of recognition was informal (it's not like they handed out trophies every week, they just sent out a note to recognize people's good performance).

Some examples of informal rewards are:

MANAGERS PERSONALLY RECOGNIZE EMPLOYEES

This shows people that their managers and supervisors see them, and they recognize what they're doing for the company.

MANAGERS WRITE PERSONAL NOTES ABOUT GOOD PERFORMANCE

Practically nobody handwrites notes anymore, although they can feel more heartfelt than an email. Having said that, an email does do the trick here. Bonus points if you copy the executive team on the message.

MANAGERS RECOGNIZE EMPLOYEES PUBLICLY FOR PERFORMANCE

Too many managers focus on private recognition, which can be helpful, but people want to feel the pride of being recognized in public. They want to feel special—they crave it. Give them an opportunity to bask in that pride.

MANAGERS HOLD TEAM MEETINGS TO CELEBRATE SUCCESSES

It's even more powerful to be recognized in your team specifically, where people have a more intimate context of your contributions.

There are no cons to using these forms of informal rewards. These are no-cost actions that have significant positive impacts on people. Even if your rewards budget is $0, there's still no excuse not to take some of these actions into consideration.

- **Have the CEO thank them for a good job**—we find that it's even more effective when you have the president, CEO, or other head of the organization make this call or write a handwritten thank you note to the employee.
- **Make it specific**—just telling someone they did a good job isn't helpful, because they may not know what they're being recognized for. Make sure to tell them specifically what they did to earn the praise they're receiving.

LOW-COST REWARD IDEAS

CREATE AN OUT-TO-DINNER PROGRAM FOR EMPLOYEES

A "dinner on us" gift certificate so the employee and their spouse can share the reward is a great idea. That brings the reward home, which has a powerful impact.

GIVE A PERSONALIZED GIFT RELATED TO AN EMPLOYEE'S HOBBY OR INTEREST

This is another powerful one if you get it right. One manager I know runs a warehouse where several of the employees play video games. The manager keyed into that, because he heard them talking about it in the warehouse. So when the whole group was excited about a video game's upcoming release, the manager went out and bought the game for each of his employees. Even though it only cost that manager a few hundred dollars, the camaraderie and respect that it fostered was worth far more. When you give a personalized gift like this, it tells your employees that you know them, you know what they like, and that you care about their lives outside of work.

TICKETS TO EVENTS

A lot of companies default to sporting events, but you don't have to do that. If you know a certain employee likes the theatre or the opera, you should personalize the gift to match that interest. The more you cater to their interests with the rewards, the more powerful they become, even if they are relatively low-cost.

CONTRIBUTION TO CHARITY

Making a contribution to a charity in the employee's name can be incredibly meaningful to some employees, and completely meaningless to others. Choose wisely.

PROFESSIONAL MEMBERSHIP AND TRAINING

These options are great for people who are close to reaching a promotion and need just a little boost to reach that next level.

MONEY

Cash is king when it comes to employee rewards. I've talked to a lot of employees who get a plaque or trophy, and while they appreciate it, they say after the fact, "You know, I just wish they'd given me the cash they spent on this plaque." Let's put it this way: nobody will ever deny cash.

A good rule of thumb is to give out cash rewards in private. Doing it in public does not go over well with the team, and it embarrasses the employee, which can taint the experience.

TIME OFF

This reward is second only to cash in terms of effectiveness. The time off could be as short as an extra break or a longer lunch, but it could be as long as a day off, a three-day weekend, or an entire week off. Again, this is another reward I don't see utilized as much as it should be. A lot of organizations bristle against this concept, saying it's too expensive to give people extra time off, but that's completely wrong. Not only do employees really appreciate time off, but what happens is they wind up coming back more refreshed than before, and they will actually be more motivated. It's ironic: the more time people take off, the more productive they'll be.

GROWTH AND ADVANCEMENT

People love getting more responsibility, especially if they're trying to get a promotion. A lot of managers don't see it that way. They think if they give people more responsibility, they have to give them more money, and that isn't always true. If you think back to our job evaluations, you'll remember that you have to give people a tremendous amount of responsibility before they can move to the next level of their job. Therefore, if you communicate with someone that you want to help them gain more experience with the added responsibility, which can help them advance in their career, that can be a reward in itself.

RESPONSIBILITY AS REWARD

A great example of this might be a human resources employee. Let's say this person spends their time recruiting people all day every day, and their manager recognizes that they have tremendous people skills. The manager might say, "You know, I've noticed that you're a great recruiter. You're doing great with interviewing, screening, and making job offers. I want you to get involved with some internal employee relations." That means when an employee has issues with a manager, this human resources employee can be a mediator between the two. That affords the employee the opportunity to learn a new skill, more visibility for their role, and a better opportunity to advance.

On the other hand, this can go too far as well. If that person was spending forty hours a week, day in and day out, doing recruiting stuff, adding another twenty hours a week worth of employee relations work would be too much. At that point, you'd be abusing what should be a reward and turning it into an exploitation.

MERCHANDISE REWARDS

These are much more common and can be mid-range in cost. Some ideas include:

- Electronics.
- Productivity tools, such as software or supplies.
- Customized organization logo gifts.
- Spa visits, massages, babysitting services.

CELEBRATIONS

These are more for the entire group, and celebrations don't necessarily have to reward a specific good deed. They can be more of a standard, regular celebration of the team in general.

ORGANIZATION OUTINGS

Company outings can be a huge part of the culture. It's a chance for people to bond and connect outside of the workspace.

SPECIAL DAYS AND MONTHS

You can also celebrate special months or days, such as Black History Month, Earth Day, or Heart Month.

FUN CONTESTS AND TREASURE HUNTS

I worked with one scientific organization where they celebrated Pi Day on March 14. The executive team bought pies and had employees throw them at their faces in the cafeteria, and all the money they raised went to charity.

STAFF BIRTHDAYS

These celebrations can bring the organization together and encourage everyone to have fun.

FOOD AT CELEBRATIONS

Now, this is a personal preference of mine, but I want you to consider this. When I advise companies, I advise them not to make their celebrations center around food (unless, of course, you're throwing a pie in someone's face). It might sound odd, but I'll tell you a story that will show you why.

One organization I worked with centered every gathering around food. Every birthday party had cake, every team meeting had pizza, and every outing was fully catered. When people left the company, in the exit interview I asked them what negatives they experienced working at the company. Almost without fail they all said:

"I gained a lot of weight working here."

Seriously. Some people gained close to fifty pounds because their celebrations were frequent and they all centered around food. That's not good. It flies in the face of wellness and health.

So of course feel free to have your celebrations center around food, but if you choose unhealthy options (like pizza and cake), just know that over time, those choices will add up. Healthy foods would be better for you and your employees; they stay healthy, and your health insurance premiums stay low.

EMPLOYEE AWARDS

These can take the form of financial rewards, public recognition, or some combination of both.

- Employee Excellence Award.
- Quality Achievement Award.
- Employee Suggestion Award.

- Customer Service Award.
- Employee of the Month Award.
- Employee Safety Award.
- Team Award.
- President's Award.

EMPLOYEE SERVICE AWARDS

These are generally anniversary awards for when people have been with the company for five years, ten years, fifteen years, and beyond.

SPECIAL EVENTS AND TRAVEL AWARDS

If someone does particularly well, you can reward them by sending them and their family on a trip out of town.

ORGANIZATION STOCK OWNERSHIP

From what I've seen, this is a very successful reward program. When people are awarded with stock, they feel like an owner, and it gives them a powerful and concrete incentive to improve the organization.

HEALTH AND WELLNESS

Creating programs around health can encourage people to live a healthy lifestyle, especially if you give them a formal reward for succeeding at it. Walking contests are a particularly popular health reward.

SOCIAL RESPONSIBILITY

This can take a few forms: you can reward your employees with time off for volunteerism, or you can reward them for their work by matching their contributions to their favorite charity.

TAKE YOUR PICK

I've given you a ton of ideas in this chapter. They're all useful, but you may feel overwhelmed looking at all of them. How do you choose which programs are best for you and your organization?

You have to pick which options fit the situation, the employees, and your budget. If you're financially constrained, stick with the no-cost and low-cost rewards and milk those for all they're worth.

From what I've seen, many organizations are so lax with rewarding employees that if you just do that, you'll be ahead of 90 percent of them.

For the higher cost items (anything over $200), I have a suggestion:

Set aside 0.5 percent of your payroll budget for big-ticket reward items such as time off, cash, and celebrations.

Depending on the size of your organization, that may be a significant part of your budget. But I've seen what happens when you do this process consciously and thoughtfully. If you put together a program using both informal low-cost rewards and formal higher-cost rewards, you'll see a more engaged workforce. People will feel like they're being recognized, and they'll be more likely to work hard and stay with your company.

Recognition is a basic need for people, and far too many companies don't fulfill that need. If you buck the trend and show your people how much you appreciate them, you'll keep your employees connected, interested, and motivated.

CHAPTER 10

8

INCORPORATING INCENTIVES

EVERYTHING YOU NEED TO KNOW ABOUT VARIABLE PAY PROGRAMS

In the last chapter, we discussed recognition and rewards. Now we're going to move up to the next level of rewards: variable pay programs.

Variable pay programs are incentive plans that allow employees to achieve mutually agreed upon goals to potentially increase their compensation. In this chapter, I'm going to teach you the different types of incentive plans for employees, and I'll give you some ideas for what performance measures to track, and how to design an effective incentive plan.

I like to focus on six types of incentive programs:

- Spot awards.
- Short-term plans.
- Long-term plans.
- Individual incentives.
- Group incentives.
- Enterprise incentives.

Let's start with the simplest incentives...

SPOT AWARDS

Similar to the rewards we discussed in chapter 9, one-time project awards can serve as an incentive for an employee's extraordinary contributions. As opposed to many of the rewards we talked about earlier—which might simply be a plaque or a trophy—these spot awards are comprised of cash, ranging in the thousands of dollars.

You can manage this by giving the managers a certain budget allotment every year for spot awards to be distributed at their discretion.

SHORT-TERM INCENTIVE PLANS

These plans are tracked for a year or shorter, and they have objectives that your employees need to feel in control of or have significant influence over. In other words, the objectives need to be achievable, easy to measure, and have a concrete impact on the organization.

These can be profit-sharing-based incentives or commission-based (which we'll discuss later).

LONG-TERM INCENTIVE PLANS

These incentive plans last longer than a year (typically three to four years), and they have a longer line of sight because the decisions employees make to reach these incentives have higher financial impacts over the long-term.

Most often, it's executives who are involved with these long-term plans because they're more involved with long-term decisions. In fact, you don't even want executives on a short-term incentive plan without a long-term plan because you don't want them making short-term decisions.

These can be in the form of deferred cash, stock options, or performance shares.

MILESTONE INCENTIVE PLANS

I covered much of this in chapter 9, but this refers to any small dollar value spot awards for reaching milestones or technical achievements. Milestone bonuses, in particular, have a lot of incentive power because they get people to cross the finish line with their projects.

For projects that have a strict timeline, timing milestones with small cash rewards are very effective (for example, they get a $1,000 bonus for finishing the first third of the project on time, another bonus for finishing the second third on time, and another bonus for completion of the whole project on time).

TECHNICAL ACHIEVEMENT AWARDS

These can range anywhere from $3,000 to $5,000. Typically only science and tech organizations offer technical achievement awards (especially for patents and invention bonuses), but they can be effective in any organization. Your company gets the benefit of higher output and better performance, and the employee gets the benefit of more pay—it's win-win, and I encourage you to use these types of incentive plans widely.

GROUP AND TEAM INCENTIVE PLANS

These incentive plans promote a group effort, where either all managers or all individual contributors get a group bonus for meeting a group milestone. I recommend that this payout be in the form of equity, such as stock options, restricted stocks, or appreciation rights.

STOCK PURCHASE PLANS

If you are in a publicly-traded organization, employees can often purchase stock at a discount. If it's a successful company, people can keep buying company stock and use that as a vehicle to build wealth. I've seen that at a lot of large corporations where, over time, people build a lot of wealth because they keep buying stock.

I saw this happen at Hewlett-Packard; people who worked on the assembly line for decades participated in the stock purchase program and retired as multimillionaires. Now, everything does have to line up for this to work: you have to offer the program, the participant has to buy the stock, and the company has to be successful. This doesn't work for, say, an Enron-type company. It's hard to get everything to line up for an enterprise-wide incentive program like discount stock purchasing. But when it does, you allow everyone in your organization to achieve the American dream.

HOW TO DECIDE WHICH INCENTIVE PLAN TO USE

How do you decide which incentive plan to put in place? I suggest you start by asking yourself a few questions to find out:

DO YOU ALREADY HAVE A BASE COMPENSATION PROGRAM IN PLACE?

If you don't have a base salary program in place already—where you're paying relative to the market rates—it won't do you much good to add an incentive plan on top of that. Get the fundamentals right before you tack on an incentive plan.

THREE COMPANIES, NO PLAN

I worked with a young entrepreneur who owned three companies, and he loved creating incentive plans. But year after year they failed, so he reached out for help. I asked him what the problem was.

He said, "These incentive plans don't really create the behaviors I'm looking for from my employees. I still have a ton of turnover. What should I do?"

"Well, let's start with the basics. When was the last time you reviewed your base compensation plan?"

"Oh, I don't care about that," he said.

"I know it's more fun to focus on incentives, and it's a lot of work to get your base program right, but that has to come first. If you aren't paying people appropriately from the start, it's not going to work."

But he didn't listen, and all of his companies have suffered as a result.

CAN YOU MEASURE WHAT YOU'RE DOING?

If you can't measure your incentive plan's objectives, then it's not going to work.

DO THE PARTICIPANTS HAVE CONTROL OVER THE RESULTS?

If they don't have control over the results, they won't be incentivized to improve.

IS THE ENVIRONMENT STABLE?

If your financial situation is unstable, and you're up one year and down the next, the inconsistency will not incentivize people. It'll just make them more anxious.

DOES YOUR TOP MANAGEMENT TEAM SUPPORT THESE INCENTIVES?

Without their support, the plan can easily fail. For one of my clients, I worked with the CFO and head of human resources to put together an amazing incentive plan that took months of work. When we brought it to the CEO, he laughed at us and said, "This is exactly what I didn't want."

The CFO, head of HR, and I looked at each other and felt our hearts break. We had to go back to the drawing board and undo months of hard work. I wanted to be mad at the CEO, but really it was our own fault. We didn't involve him from the outset, and if we had, we could have gotten his input and had buy-in from everyone.

Also ask yourself:

- Do you have the staff to support and administer an incentive plan?
- Do you have data integrity?
- Can your business processes handle the results of incentive plan success?

A FEW THINGS TO DO WHEN YOU CREATE AN INCENTIVE PLAN

- Clearly understand why you are creating the plan.
- Determine the purpose and objective of the plan.
- Involve others in the plan design—just like my example with the CEO nixing our plan, the process may be more important than the actual plan.
- Be clear about who is eligible—about 60 percent of organizations have incentive plans where everybody's eligible, which I think is the way to go.
- Select the right performance measures.
- Figure out plan funding—is the plan self-funded? That's music to a CFO's ear. I suggest you lay out an analysis of exactly how much productivity these plans will create and how much revenue that will bring in relative to the incentives.
- Create achievable target plan payouts and criteria— you have to decide if your payout is all or nothing, or if people can reach part of the target and get a partial payout. I discourage you from saying people have to reach 100 percent of the target or no payout. It should not be all or nothing, because that leads to demotivation. Also, I do not recommend capping incentive plans, including for sales. Think about it; if you cap incentives, once people reach that cap, they're no longer rewarded for going above and beyond, so why would they?
- When I ask CFOs why they want to cap incentive plans, they usually say they don't want people to get too much

of a windfall and hurt the company's bottom line. I want to smack the calculator out of their hand when they say that. You do realize that if your incentive plan is designed well, a windfall for your employee is also a windfall for your organization, right?

· Reserve the right to amend the plan—I recommend assessing these plans on a regular basis. Seriously. Always maintain the integrity of the plan, but if some external factor comes in and impacts your bottom line, you need to reassess. Keep the integrity of the plan, but keep the targets realistic relative to the economy and your business.

A FEW THINGS NOT TO DO WHEN YOU CREATE AN INCENTIVE PLAN

DON'T CREATE A TECHNICAL SOLUTION TO SOLVE A CULTURAL PROBLEM

Here's what I mean by that: I worked with an organization of about three hundred employees. They had an incentive plan that was only eligible to people who had the word "director" in their title. If you didn't have director in your title, you couldn't get the incentives.

All of a sudden, a third of the company—literally one hundred out of three hundred people—were directors.

The CEO came to me and said, "We have too many people on the incentive plan."

No duh, I thought. People's actual results weren't driving them to join the incentive program or getting a director title. It was simply being handed out like Halloween candy.

We had to do a market analysis to decide which jobs—*not* which people—should be part of the incentive plan based on their job content.

I brought the data to the CEO. He said, "This still doesn't solve my director problem."

"Here's an easy solution right now: take the director title away from everyone. Tell everyone that only board members are called directors, and now everybody has functional titles."

In the end, a lot of people had to be taken off the incentive program, which wasn't pleasant, but it was a product of their own creation for inflating the number of directors they had in the organization. Which brings me to the next *don't*...

DON'T OVERCOMPLICATE THE PLAN

Having too many measurements for your incentive plan leaves employees wondering how they're doing. I worked with a CEO who used twelve metrics to measure his incentive plan. Why? Because they were the twelve metrics the board of directors was basing *his* incentive plan on. I told him that would create too much anxiety for his employees because it was too complex.

Keep it to three to five metrics.

DON'T LET THE INCENTIVE PLAN BECOME AN ENTITLEMENT

Give progress reports to let employees know how they're doing relative to your plan metrics. You don't want people thinking they're entitled to incentives. Make sure they're looking at the objectives and working hard to reach them.

DON'T MISS ANY PAYOUTS

You will see nothing kill morale faster than failing to pay out an incentive plan. That's the kind of mistake that causes people to leave. And ironically, the people who would leave would be the high achievers—the ones who would have otherwise reached their incentive bonuses.

HOW TO DETERMINE INCENTIVE PLAN REQUIREMENTS

Every incentive plan you create must be designed and targeted to a unique business challenge your organization is facing. The correlation between the incentive plan measurements and the business challenge must be so clear that when you ask your employees what it is, they know it.

You must all work as a team. One-size-fits-all will not work. You can't measure success the same for your production team as your customer service team. You have to collaborate with each group to figure out the most important objectives for them and spell them out explicitly in the incentive plan.

It's a lot of work, but it looks like this:

- Spell out the overall financial objectives for the organization.
- Use those organizational objectives to determine department objectives.
- Use those department objectives to spell out individual objectives.

There's a lot of work involved, so you have to test it out and modify it, because business conditions change, departments change, and people change. Again, you should adjust your incentive plan constantly.

> Make sure you have a high-level view so you don't create an incentive plan that disrupts or cancels out another.

HOW TO MEASURE INCENTIVE PLAN SUCCESS

Every incentive plan must be customized with its own measures of success. Any of these improvements are a potential marker that an incentive plan is working:

- Lower cost per unit produced.
- Higher revenue and profit per unit or service.
- Increased sales and market share.
- Company equity and stock value appreciation.
- Improved profitability.
- Improved company value or more capital for expansion.

A few other examples of financial returns on incentive programs are: improved speed of product delivery, improved quality of product or service, reduced overhead expenses, and increased sales per representative.

HOW TO MARKET PRICE INCENTIVES

Now, you don't want to just throw awards out there randomly, even if you are the CFO of labor cost. The *other* CFO will find you and hurt you if you do because you'll inevitably go over budget. By the same token, you don't want your payouts to be so low that they don't incentivize employees to achieve stretch (or ambitious) goals.

So what do you do? You look at survey data to set payout boundaries. Surveys will indicate the levels of bonus awards that are often tied to each level of base pay for each job. In short, in the salary survey, the recommended bonus level will be a percentage of the employee's base pay. Note that this is another reason to ensure that people's base pay is accurate, because if their base pay is too high, then you're overpaying on that plus the incentive program.

Trying to cover up a bad base pay program with incentive programs is like trying to replace your kitchen appliances when you have a big hole in the roof. Take care of the fundamentals first, or else none of these other changes will matter.

THE PROBLEM WITH FLAT INCENTIVES

Some organizations like to do flat amounts—say $5,000—but that doesn't work because different jobs have different levels of responsibility, and therefore should have different levels of incentive payouts.

INCENTIVE PLAN ADMINISTRATION

Processing payouts in a timely and accurate manner is a huge problem with incentive plans, and failing to do so can kill the momentum of the plan and lose the goodwill of employees. You should have a system set up that monitors progress toward incentives and gives regular reports to employees.

Some questions to consider when administering your plan:

Do you still pay out incentives if employees are no longer employed with you?

Do you still pay out if they are on discipline?

Do you prorate the plan payout for a new employee?

If an employee passes away mid-year, do their beneficiaries get a payout?

Is the payout subject to a 401k match or taxes?

You need to answer these questions for your own plan. I recommend having your legal counsel give you an approved boilerplate for every incentive plan so you can amend it for each department.

WHERE DOES THE SALES TEAM FIT IN THE EQUATION?

I want to talk about sales compensation with the rest of the incentive plans because, in a way, a salesperson's commission is a form of incentive compensation. But it has some unique elements that warrant a separate discussion.

SOME CONSIDERATIONS

Eligibility—consider how you define your sales force

because once people see the sales commission incentives, everyone who touches the sales cycle will want a piece of the action. Sales can be very lucrative, and people know that.

For example, if you're a customer service rep taking care of all the people the outside sales reps brought in, you may be wondering why you aren't getting any of the cut. My suggestion is to cap the sales commission eligibility at outside sales reps; otherwise, everyone and their grandmother will want a piece of that commission.

TARGET CASH COMPENSATION

With outside sales reps, you're not looking at only base salary. Because commission is such a big part of their complete compensation, you have to look at the plan mix to see the percentage of base salary versus incentive you have. If most salespeople in your organization get 60 percent of their compensation from base salary and 40 percent of their compensation from incentives, that's a 60/40 pay mix.

The higher the percentage of their compensation comes from incentives (in this case, commissions), the more they'll be driven to make sales.

PAYOUT CYCLES

You have to decide if you'll pay out your commissions on a

monthly or quarterly basis. It would be unusual to pay out on an annual basis for sales commissions because that's salespeople's bread and butter, and if they have to wait until the end of the year to get it, they won't be happy.

TWO TYPES OF SALES INCENTIVE PLANS

Commission	Bonus
Predeterminded dollar amount for each unit	Usually a percentage of base pay
Intense focus on sales volume	May have multiple objectives to achieve
May be difficult to forcast sales units	Recognizes territory variations
Salesperson has significant influence on customer decision	Confident in ability to forecast and set goals
	Shared influence

Commission-Based

A commission-based plan pays out a predetermined dollar amount for each unit or service they sell. So every time they sell a widget, they know they get a $100 commission, for example. This allows them to have an intense focus on sales volume, but it may make it difficult for you to forecast their sales of units. In this type of plan, the salesperson has significant control over the sales process because they know exactly how much they'll be compensated for a sale.

Bonus-Based

This type of incentive plan usually pays out a percentage of the salesperson's base pay. This plan also takes into account territory variations. Here's what I mean: things get testy when you give people sales territories. Let's say you have a rep in Iowa who has to drive two hours to visit a customer, and a rep in New York City who could visit ten customers in that amount of time. You have to work out how you'll pay them both equitably because you'll find that the reps in more rural markets will get bitter towards the city-based reps who clean house in their territories.

WHY AM I PAYING MY SALESPEOPLE A BASE SALARY *AND* COMMISSION?

You want to communicate that their base salary is a base-line of providing customer service, so they aren't just focused on selling. The incentive plan on top of that—whether it's commission-based or bonus-based—is there to drive their sales focus. Otherwise, salespeople can get into sell-only mode and forget to take care of the customers on the other end.

A FEW THINGS TO CONSIDER FOR SALES PLANS

Again, the frequency that you pay out is important, and you may want to consider partial payouts as an advance to new sales reps, just to get the juices flowing, so to speak. You also want to decide if you want to use ceilings or caps. Personally, I think sales should be uncapped. Otherwise, people will reach a point where they're no longer motivated to sell.

Here's another consideration a lot of people don't think about: what constitutes a sale? Is it when the customer signs the contract? Is it when you ship the product? Is it when they send their payment?

There's always a conflict on this topic: the organization wants the sale to count when the customer pays the first bill. The salesperson wants the sale to count when the customer signs the agreement. It's a classic conflict. I say it should count as a sale when the customer pays their invoice—that's when the money hits the bank account. Because up until that money is in the bank, anything can happen, and you don't want to deal with taking back a commission from a salesperson.

Other considerations:

- How do you handle returns?
- Are there house accounts that get split among sales reps?
- How do you handle pricing changes in products?
- Are there team incentives?
- How do you define territories?
- What's the ramp up time (meaning when do incentives begin for new reps)?

SHOULD I USE A RAMP UP TIME FOR SALES PROFESSIONALS?

Personally, I don't like giving sales reps an early draw on their commission. Nobody comes into a sales job and is 100 percent ready to go on day one. I suggest you just increase their base salary while they're in training, then as they get into making more sales, you move away from that base salary and transition toward their normal incentive mix. That's far preferable to giving people an advance and then forcing them to pay it back.

CHAPTER 11

8

YOU'RE THE CFO OF LABOR COST

HOW TO HANDLE COMPENSATION ADMINISTRATION

Here I want to teach you how to plan and control your labor costs, including base pay, recognition, rewards, and variable pay programs like the ones we talked about in the previous two chapters. The work you've done up until this point is great, and you've collected some valuable data. But none of that hard work matters if you screw up the implementation part of the process. Here's how you do it right.

HOW TO CONTROL COSTS
VARIABLE PAY

Variable pay gives your organization more flexibility

because it is not added to base pay. This allows employees' bonuses to go up and down based on the organization's financial performance, a specific team's performance, and the individual's performance. You can hinge an employee's incentive based on certain performance metrics (which must be clearly defined and agreed upon), so you're ensured that if they get paid a certain amount, they will have produced a measurable result for the organization to earn that pay.

INHERENT COST CONTROLS

Having minimums and maximums for each salary range is an inherent cost control, and you can do the compa-ratio analysis to determine where you're paying people relative to the salary range midpoint. That way you ensure you're controlling costs by not hiring overqualified people who would require you to compensate too far above your midpoints.

You must also analyze your salary program costs. For example, if you determine based on your market analysis that you need to spend another 3 percent next year to keep your salaries at market, you need to be able to measure whether or not you're meeting that goal within budget. Because if you get this wrong—even by a half percent—and you can't afford to keep pace with the market, then it will cost your organization a lot of money—potentially millions.

CFO OF LABOR COST

If you manage the compensation in your organization, I hereby grant you the title of CFO of labor cost, because you're managing the largest expense item in the company—much larger than anything the actual CFO is managing (who of course won't like your new title, but they can handle it). And don't ask me for a promotional salary increase for managing that expense—I don't have that power; otherwise, I'd grant it to you.

I want to harp on this analysis because it's important. When people manage something as big as company-wide salaries, it's hard to take a step back and realize that messing it up might have a huge implication on everyone's livelihood. It's scary to think about. I'm encouraging you to take your time with this to figure out exactly how much it will cost to keep up with salary increases in the next year. Don't screw this up.

I've said it before, and I'll say it again: everything we've done so far leads up to this.

SALARY ADMINISTRATION POLICY STATEMENTS

What I've found is that a lot of people don't really understand a lot of salary increase verbiage, so I want to give you some common terminology to help you effectively communicate salary administration changes to your employees. Because I see this a lot: payroll managers complain about having to go back and retroactively calculate salary increases, mostly because managers delivered the increases late. It might not seem like a big deal to the managers (if anything, it seems like a hassle), but to the employees, it's a huge deal. *Do not* do retroactive salary increases.

In order to effectively communicate compensation policy statements, here is a glossary of terms that will help you in the process.

MERIT INCREASES

This means employees are eligible to receive an annual salary adjustment based on their individual performance and annual salary budget guidelines. Retroactive salary adjustments are discouraged as they impact tax withholding and payments can cross tax years.

PROMOTIONS

Promotions occur when an employee moves from a job in one grade level to a job in a higher one. Normally, an employee who is promoted will receive a pay adjustment. Other factors may include:

- The employee's current range position prior to the promotion.
- The magnitude of the change in job responsibility.

- The pay level of employees in comparable jobs.

DEMOTION

An employee may move from a job at a higher grade to a lower grade. The manager, along with human resources, should consider whether or not a salary reduction is appropriate. It's shocking how few people actually talk about this. It's as though it's a taboo subject. For instance, if an employee is struggling with their high-level job, they may schedule a meeting with their supervisor and say they want to move to a lower-level job. In that situation, what we'd do is make a plan over the course of a year or two to slowly bring that person's pay down to their new level of responsibility.

> **RED CIRCLING**
>
> In case of the organization initiating the demotion, you may red circle the employee's pay, meaning you grandfather them and keep their pay where it is, above their new job level salary, while still giving them a reduced role.

This is going to negatively impact their livelihood, so you need to sit down with them and explain it to them and work out a schedule that works for them. Show them what their salary will look like as it decreases over the coming months and years. This gives them a chance to rethink their decision if they need to; that way, they go into this with their eyes wide open.

It won't happen very often that people ask for a demotion, but when stress levels get high, it does happen.

EQUITY ADJUSTMENT

An equity increase in pay may be made to an employee's salary based on internal equity or external marketplace conditions and require review and approval by human resources. This is a challenging subject because again, a lot of states and organizations are grappling with this. You'll see a lot of equity adjustments for employees who are paid below market, and you need to go to them and say that your philosophy is to pay relative to market and you did a market study and realized that they were paid below market, so you're giving them an increase.

You can phase these out over the course of two years, depending on your budget, but no more. As slow as this process is, if you do this right, you will be doing your part to close any pay gaps. Don't wait for legislation to force your hand. Do the right thing and make equity adjustments when you find them.

LATERAL MOVES

For developmental reasons, an employee may choose to transfer to a different job at the same grade level. A lateral move may be recognized with a salary adjustment if appropriate, given the employee's position in the salary range.

I have a lot of arguments with people on this one, which is strange. People think that a lateral move doesn't deserve a reward, and that's sometimes true. But more often than not, if someone is making a lateral move (say from a level two sales job to a level two customer service job) they are increasing their compensable skills, which makes them more valuable to your organization, and worthy of a pay increase.

HIRING SALARY RATES

Managers have the discretion to offer a new hire any salary between the salary range minimum and the midpoint. Offers in excess of the midpoint are subject to the review and approval of human resources.

This is another cost-control measure. If you let managers offer in excess of the midpoint, they'll do it every time because they want to bring in high performers, even if the organization can't afford it.

SALARY RANGES

Salary ranges will be reviewed each year and adjusted as needed. Employees should not be paid below the minimum of their range. Employees normally should not be paid above the maximum of the salary range for their job, either. Salaries above the range maximum require approval by human resources.

WHEN YOU DO IT RIGHT...

If you do this salary administration part of the process correctly, you'll do wonders to contain the costs on your biggest expense: payroll. You'll not only effectively manage employees, but you'll also manage their salaries, increases, and adjustments with the grace and sophistication worthy of a CFO of labor cost.

CHAPTER 12

8

THE WORK HAS JUST BEGUN

HOW TO COMMUNICATE YOUR COMPENSATION PROGRAMS

I've said it before, and I'll say it for the millionth time. You've done a lot of work up until this point, but none of it matters if you screw up now. You have to be able to clearly communicate your compensation program to your people, you have to answer tough questions, and you have to handle giving bad news.

The first question is...

WHY DO YOU NEED TO COMMUNICATE COMPENSATION AT ALL?

Why can't you just come up with the plan, get it approved, and stop there? Why even bother communicating it to employees? The first reason is to keep people engaged. If you're transparent about how they can earn incentives, how much they'll be paid if they're promoted, and exactly what they need to do to get there, they'll be motivated, and you'll attract and retain top performers.

WHEN DO YOU COMMUNICATE ABOUT COMPENSATION?

It should be communicated first during the employee interview. That part's easy because people won't know if they want to come on board if they don't know the pay, so the compensation conversation is built in. Then it should be reiterated regularly from there: first in the employee handbook, then during regular performance reviews, and any time a change is made to the compensation plan.

Communicating compensation early and often sets concrete expectations, and it creates a transparent environment where talking about compensation is encouraged, not taboo. That way, people know exactly how much you value them from the very beginning of their working relationship with you.

WHAT TO COMMUNICATE

The first thing you should communicate is the organization's base pay philosophy, whether it's to match the market, beat it, or trail it. Then you want to communicate how the base pay is calculated (meaning you looked at the market and followed the rest of the advice in this book).

You also want to communicate any pay changes, such as market adjustments, merit increases, and pay raise and bonus criteria. And you want to let them know the value of career development opportunities, how they can impact their pay, and how benefits factor into their total compensation.

Underneath all of this, you should have relevant market data to back everything up if they're curious or skeptical.

COMMUNICATION ROLES

Everyone has a role in communicating about compensation. Let's run through everyone's obligations in the communication process.

SENIOR MANAGEMENT

Senior leaders in your organization should be setting the tone for the compensation plan. They are expected to support and "sell" the existing program to employees and act as champions of new programs. People look to senior management, and they should serve as the primary source of guidance and information for employees and supervisors.

A good senior leadership team should not say that compensation communication is the human resources arena, so they'll leave it to them. That's a cop-out. I see too many senior leadership teams who don't know anything about their compensation plans. How can they be expected to champion the plans if they don't know anything about them? Get their buy-in, and you'll get the buy-in of the whole organization.

HUMAN RESOURCES

The human resources department will be in charge of designing, implementing, and communicating the plan. They will evaluate the existing compensation programs and provide ongoing communication with the company executives so they're equipped to communicate it themselves.

Human resources teams are also in charge of providing market data to support their decisions, providing managers and employees with compensation reports, giving managers training and communication tools to discuss the plan, and designing new programs.

The human resources department should constantly be reevaluating the compensation program, looking for ways to improve it and ways to equip everyone with tools to communicate it effectively.

DESIGN TEAM

Depending on the size of your organization, you may even have a separate design team that provides input and feedback on employee communications. They act as program supporters and may include external consultants and union representatives, as well as other internal people.

DEFINE YOUR AUDIENCE

Just like any communication, you need to define your audience of compensation communication, and cater your communication to each audience. Those groups will include:

- Managers/supervisors.
- Employees.
- Union employees.
- Prospective or future employees.
- New employees.
- Family members of employees.

For all of these audiences, you need to cater your message to answer four questions:

- What's in it for them?
- What is their utmost concern?
- What questions will they have?
- How do any compensation plan changes affect them positively and negatively?

WHICH COMMUNICATION METHOD IS BEST?

I don't see a lot of people using paper-based communication anymore, which is ideal. I believe that compensation communication should be face-to-face or technology-based, though I think face-to-face is best.

These communications should be in the form of meetings, presentations, or workshops delivered from a trusted source in the organization.

But if the information is more time-sensitive, it could be delivered quickly using technology: information on the website, emails, an employee portal, videos, or even a podcast can be effective. That way, people can share, search, and access the information as needed, which is easier for them and more cost-effective for the organization.

HOW TO COMMUNICATE A NEW COMPENSATION PLAN

You'll go through three steps to communicate a new plan:

1. OBTAIN EXECUTIVE SUPPORT

First, you'll need to identify the goals of the plan, then get together with the senior management team to ensure that those goals are aligned with the business's overall goals. Then you'll provide them with a high-level overview of the proposed design, including an estimated budget and expectations for all roles.

2. OBTAIN MANAGER SUPPORT

Once you have the support of the executive team, you need to move on to the managers. When communicating the new plan to them, you'll focus less on business strategy and more on how the change will impact their employees. You can set new expectations by holding group meetings or workshops to discuss the process and timing and provide them with talking points to answer some frequently asked questions from the rest of their team.

THE MANAGER'S TOOLKIT

Be sure to give the managers a collection of tools to communicate the change to their teams, including:

- The organization compensation philosophy.
- Compensation policies.
- The new compensation structure.
- A summary of data to reinforce the changes.
- The rationale for the changes.
- Everyone in their department's salary history and performance ratings.
- Everyone's job descriptions.

3. COMMUNICATE IT TO THE EMPLOYEES

The best way to communicate the changes to employees is to have kick-off meetings presented by the management teams. These meetings should focus on a few key messages, including the plan's purpose, the mechanics and measures of the plan, the payout opportunities and participant impact, policies and procedures, and the implementation timing.

You should absolutely encourage questions during these meetings and be prepared to answer them.

As you move up and down the internal hierarchy, the basic questions you need to answer are:

What is new and/or what has changed?

Why is this change being made?

How does this change affect each of us?

How does this change affect the organization?

How does the change relate to the organization's overall mission?

Who needs to know what and when do they need to know it?

PLAN DOCUMENTS

If you distribute a plan document, it should include a few elements:

- Plan overview.
- Plan description, including:

- Performance measures.
- Administrative policies.
- How performance is measured.
- Payout frequency.
- Incentive schedule.
- How incentive earnings are calculated.
- Calculation examples—use an illustrative example to walk the employees through the process of calculating their potential incentive plan earnings.
- Administrative policies and procedures—include all terms and conditions that govern the ongoing administration of the plan, and get it reviewed by your legal team before distributing to employees. These policies and procedures might include:
  - Plan effective dates.
  - What happens in the case of employee termination/separation.
  - Eligibility timing.
  - Leaves of absence.
  - Job or territory transfers.
  - Quota or goal adjustments.
  - Sales crediting.
  - Windfall adjustments.
  - Statement of confidentiality.
- Plan agreement to be signed by employees—this shows that the participant accepts the stated performance expectations, and they abide by all the terms and con-

ditions of the plan. These signed agreements should be filed and stored electronically.

HOW TO COMMUNICATE BAD NEWS

It's not always a fun new compensation plan that you're communicating to people. Sometimes challenging financial situations call for bad news. That bad news might include wage freezes, lack of bonus-funding, salary reductions, layoffs, and more.

My advice for delivering bad news is don't sugarcoat it. Be completely open and transparent about what's happening. Involve the senior management team as well, so they can help you deliver the news early, consistently, and clearly.

Take full ownership when you deliver the news, which means you should take the time to do it in person, and consider the timing and how it will affect the person hearing the bad news. Don't do it over email, and don't do it the day before Christmas. Don't put it off on senior management, either. And for god's sake, don't blame the employee. Take the humble approach and take responsibility and encourage them to ask questions and communicate openly.

KEEP IT OPEN

The main thing I want you to take away from this chapter is to communicate openly. Whether the news is good or bad, I want compensation to be a transparent topic in your organization and in businesses everywhere. It shouldn't be taboo, because the less we talk about it, the more people are uncomfortable about it, and the more likely they are to be underpaid and unhappy. This is people's livelihood we're dealing with here, and when people don't understand why they get paid what they do, there's a disconnect between their compensation and their work. Even if you give someone a raise every year, if they don't know what they did to earn that raise, they won't be motivated, despite you paying them more. In that scenario, there's a gap between what they're getting and what they're doing to get it.

The way to bridge that gap is through communication.

CONCLUSION

A FAIR DAY'S PAY FOR A FAIR DAY'S WORK

At the beginning of this book, I said that payroll is your organization's biggest expense, and that's true. But there's another way of looking at it: payroll is your organization's biggest *investment*...and pay matters.

If you don't pay people what they're worth and communicate clearly why they're being paid that amount, that investment is not as potent as it could be...even if you pay people above market.

If you follow the advice in this book, you'll develop an infrastructure to pay people what they're worth, and that includes how they're valued inside of your organization, as well as what the external market says about their job and their individual skills. If you put all of that infrastructure together, you get an organization full of happy people who are paid what they deserve—a fair day's pay for a fair day's work.

It's a lot of work to analyze the jobs, update your job descriptions, do market analysis, figure out your salary ranges, develop your compensation and incentive programs, and communicate it to your employees, but if you don't do it, you'll be wasting your organization's biggest investment.

If you want to put your house in order, start by checking off the boxes here:

Pillar 1	Internal Consistency
☐ Job Analysis	I have collected information about the nature of specific jobs through the use of questionnaires, checklists, observation, or interviews.
☐ Job Descriptions	I have created documents that identify and describe jobs as they are currently performed.
☐ Job Evaluation	I have developed a system used to compare jobs and establish pay differences among jobs in our organization.
☐ Job Structure	I have ordered our organization's jobs from high to low based on their content or relative value to the organization.
☐ Pay Philosophy	I have established a pay policy to lead, meet, or lag the external market relative to product, industry, or people competitors.

Pillar 2	**External Competitiveness**
☐ Salary Surveys	I have participated in credible salary surveys to collect competitive market pay data.
☐ Market Analysis	I have compared internal rates of pay to external salaries to determine competitive position in the market and planned salary spending.
☐ Salary Ranges	I have created internal pay guidelines with minimum, midpoint, and maximum pay rates that approximate the salaries paid in the external market.

Pillar 3	**Employee Contributions**
☐ Performance Evaluation	I have created a pay-for-performance system, a process to determine an employee's work results against performance standards and job expectations.
☐ Increase Guidelines	I have created a process to allocate salary increase dollars based on standards, such as merit or seniority, applied consistently across individuals within the same job and organization.
☐ Incentive Programs	I have created a variable compensation program that rewards an employee for goal achievement. Forms include short-term, long-term, individual, team, and group incentive plans.

Pillar 4	**Administration**
☐ Salary Planning	I have budgeted and forecast compensation costs for the next plan year.
☐ Pay Communication	I regularly communicate to managers and employees so they understand the compensation system and how pay is determined.
☐ Program Review	I have a plan to assess the compensation program's effectiveness with managers and employees on a periodic basis.

WHERE DO WE GO NOW?

Our relationship doesn't need to end here. I want to be a resource for you. As such, I hope you'll join me in recruiting, rewarding, and retaining the best employees.

If you need compensation consulting for your organization, my team and I can assist you using the tools described in this book.

Likewise, if you need compensation training for yourself or your managers, we're here to help.

Simply email me at dweaver@comphrgroup.com for more information, connect with me on LinkedIn at linkedin.com/in/davidkweaver, or follow me on Twitter at @DavidWeaverCOMP.

ABOUT THE AUTHOR

DAVID WEAVER is president of the Compensation and HR Group and is responsible for compensation consulting within the organization. Previously, David spent twenty years managing a human resources membership organization. He has also held positions with industry leaders as a corporate human resources professional.

A graduate of the University of Massachusetts at Amherst, David has also made his mark in academia, having served as an adjunct faculty member for both Northeastern University and Newbury College, where he taught courses in Compensation Management. He is currently an instructor for the certification program at the Compensation Analyst Academy.